Family tracing

A GOOD PRACTICE GUIDE

By Lucy Bonnerjea

DEVELOPMENT MANUAL 3

Save the Children

Save the Children Development Manual No. 3

Published by
Save the Children
Mary Datchelor House
17 Grove Lane
London SE5 8RD

ISBN: 1 870322 77 0
ISSN: 0966-6982 Save the Children Development Manuals

Design and page make-up by Devious Designs
Printed by Image Offset

CONTENTS

ACKNOWLEDGEMENTS

Many people have contributed to this guide. From Angola, Nilsa de Fatima Batlha and Engracia Bento Francisco, and from Liberia Rebecca Gofan, all shared their ideas and experiences; from Mozambique, Terezinha Da Silva and Josefa Langa contributed a great deal to the discussion on planning and managing a family tracing programme, while Etelvina da Cunha, Aderito Ismael and Joana Simao shared their experiences of day-to-day tracing. In Ethiopia, Molla Asnake spent many late nights discussing the family tracing programme of Wollo and the continuing need for family tracing in Ethiopia today. My first and my last visits were to Uganda, where Fred Kasozi taught me an immense amount about the complexities of family tracing in war, while Juliet Muhumuza travelled to the four corners of the country to search out a hundred reunified children and explored their and their families' experiences of tracing and reunification. James Kabogoza shared his experiences of the complexities of long distance management and support of a programme, while Sayeed Buchena showed me how to inspect children's homes and seek out even the smallest child to ask their opinions. Within SCF, Maggie Brown, Helen Charnley and John Parry Williams were the guides and the experts, while David Tolfree and Hugo Slim provided warm and positive support. And lastly on a personal note, many thanks to Marthy and Rene who enabled me to trace the tracing systems, by looking after Benjamin.

SUMMARY

1. The aim of this guide is to draw together SCF's recent experience of family tracing. It is divided into eleven sections. The first section presents the aims of the guide and the methods. It briefly describes family tracing programmes in five countries: Angola, Ethiopia, Liberia, Mozambique and Uganda. The second section provides some historical background and looks at tracing on two different continents.

2. The third section provides an overview of the different stages of a tracing programme. It then suggests that effective tracing requires bringing together clearly developed principles and values with clearly developed logistics and systems. It is helpful to have the principles and values identified and articulated, and linked to local cultural values as well as international conventions. Tracing systems also need a clear specification of roles and the prioritisation of record keeping.

3. The fourth section addresses the identification of children with tracing needs and discusses who should do tracing (specialist versus generalist teams) and how it should be done. It argues for a national education programme on tracing.

4. The fifth section examines the documentation process and argues that it involves creating a social history but also a diagnostic tool for the child and the adult to choose a plan for the child's future. There are many obstacles to doing this successfully. Then the next step is to record the history and the plan: forms, questions, photographs and computers are discussed as tools.

5. The sixth section, on tracing, argues that different situations require different tracing methods. Tracing with children present is not good practice and should if possible be avoided. Preparation, discussion and listening to fears remains important in communicating with both children and families. Verification of the family is the next step, followed by an assessment of the family's social and economic situation.

6. The seventh section, on family reunification, suggests that it involves re-creating a family rather than returning to a previous situation. Safeguards need to be built into reunifications and often after care also needs to be provided. There are also occasions where reunification is not, after all in the best interests of a child and alternative placements are needed. Substitute family placements may be preferable to dumping children where neither they nor their families want them.

7. The eighth section argues for the importance of follow-up work as well as more formal evaluations. The ninth section identifies the importance of staff motivation and management as key criteria for success. The guide then looks at some aspects of the politics of partnership between governments and NGO funders in the tenth section. Finally, in the eleventh section, it looks at family tracing in non-emergency social development.

INTRODUCTION

WHAT DOES FAMILY TRACING MEAN?

Children are separated, lost, kidnapped and abandoned during times of war, drought, migration, population displacements – or extreme poverty. Family tracing is the process of attempting to reunite children with their families, and can involve a number of different activities, including:

- the search for parents and relatives to return the children to;
- the search by families for the children who have been lost;
- the search for long-term living situations for children, if family reunification proves impossible.

The term 'family tracing' is used in this guide as a term for all the activities involved in what is formally known as Identification, Documentation, Tracing and Reunification programmes (IDTR). IDTR is the more accurate description. Family tracing is however a more understandable term which also embraces alternative placements.

THE DIFFICULTIES OF FAMILY TRACING

Family tracing may sound simple until one remembers that in many wars millions of people are displaced and many parents, when traced, are dead. The children are sometimes too frightened to tell where they were living and often cannot tell where the parents might be if they are alive. Even if relatives are found, judgments have to be made about whether to return children to unsafe areas or areas where there is little or no food. Judgments also have to be made about whether children can safely be allowed to choose where they live and what to do if the choice is not the same as that of their relatives. Tracing, or searching for family, often means setting off into the unknown, in landrovers, trekking across mountains on mules, walking for days and coming back with no news or bad news.

This setting off into the unknown is done by each of the parties involved in family tracing: families, governments, international non-governmental organisations (NGOs) and the International Committee of the Red Cross

(ICRC), the intergovernmental organisation in international tracing. Families and communities try to trace through traditional leaders, elders, churches and relatives. Governments try and incorporate tracing into their basic concern to aid the survival of the population – with food and curative health care. And NGOs may start a tracing programme to respond to large numbers of visibly separated children – or may be tracing as part of other work such as working with street children or trying to heal the traumas of war.

It is rare for any of these parties (except the ICRC) to have past experience of tracing and the learning curve is long and slow. The casualties of this slow learning are the many children whose families cannot be traced because, over time, all links to the past disappear; the children who are placed in situations which are damaging to them and add more pain to the loss they have already suffered; the children who cross the invisible line of becoming 'too old' to reunify, perhaps because they have learnt the survival skills of the city or the camps and cannot adapt these to the villages.

THE AIM OF THIS GUIDE

The aim of the guide is to draw together some recent experiences of family tracing and to disseminate the learning from these experiences. The guide is primarily for three target audiences:

- for planners and practitioners, who may be setting up new IDTR programmes following wars or disasters;
- for planners and practitioners already working in IDTR programmes who may wish to know about other experiences so they can review their own;
- for planners and practitioners who may wish to apply some of this experience to working with children separated from their families in other, non-war situations (for example street children).

By recording some of the aims, methods and experiences of recent tracing activities this guide will help with family tracing both for children who are searching for their families, and families who are searching for their children, in any part of the world, wherever they get separated. All countries have traditional, informal, oral tracing systems and formal tracing systems need to build on and strengthen these: community leaders and community networks are the key in both informal and formal systems of family tracing.

But no two wars or droughts are the same, and no two tracing systems are the same either. As a result this is not a prescriptive manual but rather a collection of ideas, principles and experience to adapt and use flexibly and imaginatively in current and future situations, with the emphasis on good practice and best practice.

THE BUILDING BLOCKS OF THIS GUIDE: EXAMPLES FROM FIVE COUNTRIES

The idea for this guide grew out of Save the Children's involvement in family tracing in five countries over the last ten years. By reviewing the tracing that took place in those five countries and examining the methods used, SCF sought to establish some of the impacts of these, and to draw out any lessons which could be learned. The five countries involved were Angola, Ethiopia, Liberia, Mozambique and Uganda.

The review had three principal dimensions:

- First, it attempted to establish how tracing had evolved and developed in each of the countries and what could be learnt from each.
- Second, it attempted to look at the similarities and differences in tracing methods and outcomes between the different countries.
- Third, while most of the review examined the work funded by Save the Children in the five countries, the work of the respective governments and other partner NGOs was also considered. The work was carried out over a six-month period during 1993.

Angola

The Family Tracing Project in Angola began in 1990. The project aims to trace the families of children who have been separated through war and to create a series of alternatives for care in the community for children whose families cannot be traced or who cannot care for them. Six hundred and fifty children have been reunited in three years; there are a further two thousand living in government homes and many more in substitute homes. The number of separated children is rising due to the resumption of hostilities.

Childcare teams consisting of government personnel were established through training seminars. However, in 1993 only a third of these were still operating due to the effects of the war on certain provinces. Their role was to trace families where possible; to identify and interview potential adoptive parents and foster parents; to offer some long-term planning for children who had been separated for a long time. The teams work with religious organisations, the Red Cross, and traditional chiefs.

SCF's role has been twofold: to provide technical assistance in setting up and developing a tracing programme; and to provide financial assistance. SCF works in two provinces, and at the national level. No other international NGO works directly on tracing of children.

Ethiopia

At the outbreak of the 1983–85 famine, SCF opened up three emergency feeding shelters in Wollo where tens of thousands of people were fed. As climatic conditions improved, families left for their villages, and some two and a half thousand unaccompanied children were 'discovered' left at the shelters. A reunification programme was designed with the Ethiopian Relief and Rehabilitation Commission. Ten 'auxiliaries' – staff who were already working in the shelters – were trained, and their tasks included: interviewing and registering each child; tracing families and explaining to communities why reunification was important; weighing children and monitoring their health; returning children; following up children.

Distances were great and tracing involved expensive flights to remote areas as well as travel by horse, mule and days of walking. The use of local staff who knew the children was important, as was the direct involvement of the local party committees, the government and mass organisation leaders in tracing, verifying families and monitoring the children after reunification. The majority of children were reunited and some two hundred were left for alternative placements. SCF's role was organisational and financial, and was particularly important in getting the project off the ground. However, the local evaluation concluded: 'It is difficult if not impossible for expatriates to run such a programme.' *

Liberia

In Liberia, Save the Children, the Liberian Red Cross Society, the Orphaned and Abandoned Children, the Children Assistance Programme, the ICRC, UNICEF and other organisations have all been working with the Ministry of Health and Social Welfare, setting up shelters for abandoned and separated children and developing tracing programmes associated with them.

Many of the children saw the physical killing of parents and relatives, and other acts of violence, while others were forced to join in and fight at the battle front. Many of these children were traumatised, orphaned and

---

* Molla Asnake: 'SCF (UK) Orphan Reunification Programme', Wollo/ Ethiopia. SCF 1987

abandoned. The Small Boys Union (SBU) of the National Patriotic Front of Liberia (NPFL) has been encamped outside of Monrovia undertaking a trauma healing programme. All of these children need help tracing their relatives. There is a further group of children who fled the country but wish to come back, who are being helped under the Repatriation and Resettlement Programme set up in 1991.

Workshops are organised for all these various groups prior to and after resettlement. Much of the tracing work was initiated by NGOs at a time when there was no recognised government, but this has changed and NGOs are now working more closely with the present government.

Mozambique

Mozambique's family tracing programme arose as a result of the thousands of children separated from their families during the war of destabilisation. Though the vast majority of these children were cared for in the community by neighbours or other substitute families it was considered important to reunify children with their own families whenever possible.

As a result of national seminars in 1983, 1985 and 1987, the National Directorate of Social Action had already formulated a policy of non-institutional care aimed at reinforcing traditional community-based care. Following locally-based initiatives the national family tracing programme began in 1988 with a training course for social action staff, workers from the Organisation of Mozambican Women and various NGOs. This course was based around the needs of a group of children who had been kidnapped and later freed.

Training courses were then carried out in Mozambique's ten provinces for government workers, community leaders and volunteers involved in the implementation of the programme. The programme receives financial and technical support from three international NGOs: Redd Barna, SCF (US) and SCF (UK) as well as the Christian Council of Mozambique.

Although the Mozambican family tracing programme was created in response to an emergency situation, a continuing need for identification, documentation, tracing and reunification activities is anticipated during the repatriation of refugees and the resettlement of internally displaced populations.

Uganda

A long history of civil war led here too to massive population displacements, and eventual attempts by the ICRC to return people to their villages. Children however were taken to transit camps in Kampala where they were vulnerable to many abuses. There are many tales of people queuing at these camps for houseboys and housegirls; some NGOs are even said to have used this route to cheap labour.

Tracing was the programme set up to empty these camps of children, and to offer them the protection of a family environment. The Ministry of Social Welfare seconded a member of staff to SCF who developed a programme of tracing, using information on clans, totems and so on. Several thousand families were traced and children returned.

At the same time, many children's institutions were set up during the war in the 1980s. Some were motivated by the wish to protect children; others were attracted by the opportunity to earn money through eliciting donations for 'orphans' from overseas contacts, particularly overseas churches. Some of the children were orphans; others were placed in institutions by parents whose poverty prevented them from educating their children. It is estimated that there are some seventy homes in existence, housing nearly three thousand children.

Following the tracing from transit camps, the children's institutions came under scrutiny, with a national survey demonstrating very low standards of food and care. As a result the 'Children's and Babies' Homes' Rules were drawn up and put before Parliament in 1991. These required homes to register and meet certain standards, and these standards included family tracing. Finally, the most recent situation in which tracing is used is to attend to the growing HIV/Aids problem – where family placements are sought for 'Aids orphans' as an alternative to institutional care.

Methodology

The fieldwork for this guide was carried out during 1993.

The methodology consisted of interviews with staff, observation of tracing and reunification, and two pieces of commissioned research. In more detail, this involved the following:

- Interviews took place with government staff from all five countries who were involved in planning and implementing tracing programmes. These included Ministry staff with overall responsibility for the programmes as well as district and provincial level staff who were carrying out the individual tracings and reunifications. SCF staff were interviewed from all the countries. In Ethiopia and Mozambique interviews were carried out with other international NGOs. A workshop was held which brought together nationals from the five countries to share experiences.

- Observation of tracing and reunification took place in Uganda and in Mozambique.
- In Mozambique a survey of social work staff was carried out. This was a postal questionnaire based on initial interviews in two provinces. In Uganda a survey of resettled children and their families was also carried out. A hundred children were identified from records of reunification in six different districts and a researcher was appointed to interview the children, the families and the community leaders separately for each reunification. This is also used in this guide to illustrate both the successes and the difficulties of family tracing.

PAST TRACING

Children have become separated from their families in virtually every war, famine, population displacement, migration, disaster or refugee situation. The best published review of the circumstances and consequences of such separation for children is by Ressler, Boothby and Steinbock in *Unaccompanied Children: Care and Protection in Wars, Natural Disasters and Refugee Movements*. This section of the guide draws heavily on examples of separation described in their review*. The aim of this section is to provide a historical context for issues of separated children and family tracing, and to broaden the focus from Africa.

Separated children are not specific to Africa, nor indeed to Third World countries. It seems important to state this, since sometimes 'family tracing' is seen as an exotic activity which is specific to Third World conditions of poverty and deprivation. Occasionally people think that large scale separation and voluntary separation of children from their families could only happen 'out there' – in poor countries. So we start in Europe, with the Second World War.

THE SECOND WORLD WAR

Every country in Europe had large numbers of orphaned or separated children by the end of the second World War. The Red Cross and Unesco both estimated that the number of orphans and abandoned children was as high as thirteen million*. After the war national social services were developed to provide for unaccompanied children and over one million children were in institutions throughout Europe. The United Nations organisations provided special services for many displaced separated children.

The thirteen million separated children included the following:
- a million or so children deported as slave labourers;
- children left alone while their parents were deported;
- children abducted for the Nazi adoption programme;
- illegitimate children of slave labourers and deportees who were not allowed to keep them;
- children who were accidentally separated;
- children hidden and moved to safety by parents.

Family tracing, called the 'child search program' in 1945, was originally designed for the 'location, documentation and repatriation of Allied separated children'*. Good practice was slow to evolve. Initially child-search workers visited homes and institutions and had the right of search and seizure; they abruptly removed many children who had no knowledge of their origins. They were housed in transit camps in some distress. Gradually a policy developed of registering children but allowing them to stay in their foster or adoptive homes until their parents were located. And then finally the policy changed: it moved away from automatic repatriation to 'determining the best interests of the child and the child's own wishes'. In the six years from 1945, over twenty-two thousand children were located through this tracing programme.

Great Britain in the Second World War

In Britain a family separation programme was organised as a civil defence strategy in 1939 and called 'evacuation of children'.* Discussions and plans took place over a year and the separation began the day the war was declared. The separation was to be voluntary but receiving children in private homes in the rural areas was compulsory.

Half a million mothers with children under five and 750,000 school-aged children were evacuated from cities in the rural areas as protection from bombing – mostly in the first four days of the war. However, it was not considered a successful social plan: 'no sooner was the migration accomplished than its reversal began' . Three months after the start, 87 per cent of mothers with young children and nearly half of the school children had returned. The general view was that too much time had been spent on organising the logistics of the plan, such as transport and number of bedrooms available, and not enough consideration had been given either to the services needed once the children had separated or to the psychological or social consequences of the separation.

Children were also sent to Canada, the US, Australia, New Zealand – an idea that was popular with many parents. Some ten thousand were sent privately. In addition, several thousand applications were made to an organisation which was established specially to send children to Canada and the US, and two and a half thousand children were sent through them. But the scheme ended abruptly when a ship carrying children was torpedoed and sunk: the children were killed.

---

* E Ressler, N Boothby, D Steinbock: *Unaccompanied Children: Care and Protection in Wars, Natural Disasters and Refugee Movements.* OUP 1988

SOUTH EAST ASIA

Korea:

Massive social upheaval, war and the migration of large numbers of people are the main characteristics of Korea's history in the 1945–55 period. By the end of the period, more than 100,000 children were separated from their families. While in 1945 there were 38 orphanages, twenty years later there were 565 orphanages, and the number of children in them rose from three thousand to seventy thousand. After the war many of the children had been orphaned by the fighting. In the later years many were abandoned to orphanages because their parents could not feed them: only by abandoning children could parents get help. There was no large family tracing programme, but with the gradual closure of orphanages, some families reclaimed their children.

Inter-country adoption became an important alternative placement for some children in Korea. Initially this developed out of concern for illegitimate mixed race children, fathered by American soldiers, who were often abandoned and stigmatised. Many were denied schooling. International adoption programmes were set up, but widely criticised: for insufficient attention to the psycho-social effects of cross-cultural placements; for insufficient screening, selection and follow up of adoptive parents; for insufficient consideration of the circumstances under which unmarried mothers gave up their children for adoption. There was concern that more was not done to prevent separation of children, and for dealing with the problems within Korea itself. Gradually these concerns led to revisions in the adoption laws and improvements in services towards supporting poor families within Korea.

Vietnam:

The Vietnam War, like the other wars led to much death and devastation – and to many separated children. By 1973, 20,000 children lived in registered orphanages and more than 5,000 lived in unregistered ones – both in appalling conditions. Inter-country adoption became popular: numbers increased from 200 in 1970 to 1300 in 1974. Various airlifts were arranged to evacuate children – some authorised, some not – removing children, some of whom were orphans, many were not. Several thousand were flown to the US.

Some argued these separations of children from their country were humanitarian, in the best interests of the children, allowing them to survive. Others described the airlifts as kidnapping, as the taking of war souvenirs, as misdirected interventions fuelled by guilt about the war. These debates continued, with various law suits, demanding comprehensive tracing programmes to establish the full details of the families of each child removed. Tracing was, however, never systematically carried out.

OTHER DISPLACED CHILDREN

Family tracing is closely associated with wars. However, tracing is not only a tool to be used following emergency situations, but is also important in situations where children get separated as a result of extreme poverty. This includes street children, found increasingly in large cities – for example in South America – as well as child prostitution – for example minority children from Burma, China and Thailand are major victims of child prostitution. Offering help to families in these situations and negotiating the possible return of children is an important aspect of tracing and reunification work.

LESSONS FROM THE PAST: RESETTLEMENT

Reintegration should not be like the forcible resettlements practiced in history. Many of these were done for "the good of people", yet immense suffering followed. Reintegration and reunification should be a process, not an event. It should involve children, prepare them, educate them about the advantages of growing up in families, it should teach them to look long-term. It should also involve a great deal of listening to fears, assessing these and discussing these. Tracing programmes should never be known in history as the forcible resettlement of children.

WHAT IS IDTR?

EXAMPLES OF TRACING

Example 1: Waswa and Kityo were two brothers aged 12 and 8. They lived in a part of the country which was for years in the midst of the civil war. The family had to flee their village and the boys got separated from the parents. They were eventually picked up by the Red Cross and taken to an orphanage in the capital city. A year later they were included in a tracing visit to their home area. No one knew what they would find. The social worker carrying out the tracing reported: "We found that the house itself had been burnt down, but the boys recognised their elder brother, and many other relatives and village friends who could not believe that they were still alive. The excitement and congratulations were mixed with tears as they all told their sad stories."

Example 2: Kabaganda saw his parents killed and the tracing focused on trying to find his elder brother. After many days travelling, the social worker and child arrived at the boy's village. The brother had left the village many months ago. "The house was still there, but had no doors or windows, nor any sign of life. It looked like only snakes inhabited it at night time. Kabaganda wanted to stay. He went to the back of the house in the bushes, sat and wept. He was comforted but still wept all the way back. We promised we will keep checking for the brother."

Example 3: "This week's tracing exercise was a great success. We took fifteen children in the landrover, we were away for ten days, and we managed to reunite four of them. The others were brought back weeping".

These are examples of tracing in practice. The first was a successful family tracing: the children were old enough to be able to tell where they came from; they were not away for too long; and the family – what was left of it – was in the village of origin. The second was not successful. The village was located, but the family was not. The third was a success for four of the fifteen children.

OVERVIEW OF IDTR

This section provides an overview of the different stages involved in a tracing programme and argues that **Identification, Documentation, Tracing and Reunification (IDTR)** is essentially a marriage between clearly developed principles and values on the one hand and clearly developed logistics and systems on the other. Having either the principles without the systems or the systems without the principles leads to bad tracing.

Family tracing divides into four sequential stages:

Stage 1: Identification of children
Locating separated children.

Stage 2: Documenting children
Interviewing children and adults about themselves, their families and the circumstances in which they became separated.

Stage 3: Tracing Families
Searching for families and assessing whether children can be returned to them. Or publicising information about children found for families to trace them. Preparing both families and children.

Stage 4: Reunification
Returning children and setting up a monitoring system to ensure reunification is satisfactory.

PRINCIPLES AND VALUES

*"People's vision of children goes beyond the immediate family... the children are seen in terms of clan continuity and nation building. Children are like a forest planted. The old trees are cut and the new ones grow." *

Family tracing is partly a practical task, of setting budgets, organising and training tracing staff, accessing transport and fuel, and creating and maintaining records. The administration of tracing is very important. But family tracing is not the same as developing a lost property service. Clarification of the values and principles that tracing is based on is an equally important element of IDTR.

---

* P T Kakama: 'Children and their Rights: Village Perceptions'. Department of Probation and Social Welfare, Ministry of Labour and Social Affairs, Uganda 1993

The importance of family life?

Family tracing is based on the belief that, most of the time, families are best for children. Families are thought to be the best environment for the development of the child, the protection of the child, the long-term future of the child. If the parents can be found, then the reunification is a 'natural' one – it is a return of the child to the previous carers, to the biological parents who usually have a very strong social, psychological and economic bond.

If the parents cannot be found, then family tracing systems look for other relatives, starting with close relatives, which means grandparents and uncles and aunts and older siblings and then relatives who are less closely related. Matriarchal and patriarchal societies rank family members differently in order of closeness. Some societies have special relationships with uncles, or aunts or godparents. All these individual relationships operate within wider 'family' groupings, based on relationships such as clan or tribe or caste or religion. These are all ways of delineating relationships – specifying who is part of the same grouping with rights and responsibilities for each other.

Family then is neither the nuclear family unit nor necessarily the previous household unit. Family is best seen as a series of concentric circles specifying the relationship – based on blood or marriage, or even clan or religion – between people, and specifying degrees of closeness and responsibility. Where wider family tracing is done, where for example parents are known to be dead, then an understanding of degrees of closeness and responsibility is important for successful tracing.

What can the family offer? This is best seen in comparison with a non-family placement: an institution such as an orphanage, a hospital, a children-only section of a refugee camp. Families offer a place where the social skills of society are learnt, where the members share the same language and same culture, where they share an ancestry which is so important in many Third World countries. Children learn how families work, how roles are differentiated, they have social and economic models to follow. Children grow up with the same stories they heard before, the same proverbs, the same songs; they learn their age-appropriate behaviour, their rights and responsibilities and their identity as 'X's daughter' as well as their own names. They have a sense of continuity, a past that people know about, which links to the future. There is a greater sense of security and continuity and belonging.

The Rights of the Child – the UN Convention

The Convention on the Rights of the Child was adopted by the United Nations in 1989 and came into force in 1990, as the guiding document for everyone concerned with the welfare of the child. It states that the parties:

'[are] convinced that the family as a fundamental group of society and the natural environment for the growth and well-being of all its members and particularly children should be afforded the necessary protection and assistance so that it can fully assume its responsibilities within the community' ; and

'[have] recognised that the child, for the full and harmonious development of his or her personality, should grow up in a family environment, in an atmosphere of happiness, love and understanding;' and

'[believe] in all actions concerning children... the best interests of the child shall be a primary consideration' (Article 3).

The guiding principles from the Convention are:
- families are natural environments for children and may need assistance;
- children should grow up in a family environment; and
- 'the best interests' of the child should be determined in any action taken by an organisation in relation to a child.

Build on local practices and local values

The next step is to search the local context for supporting tools: what is there within the country that one is working in, that one is developing family tracing in, that suggests, through past policies, practices, customs or proverbs, that children have rights or wishes or needs?

It is a useful training exercise to brainstorm this question and to start to build up a picture of how children's policies are viewed from different angles, from different perspectives. By putting together these different understandings, this provides a direction in which to package a tracing programme.

This may involve looking at recent government policy and law on children. Or it may include, for example, taking, on an arbitrary day, a daily newspaper in a Third World city and analysing it for references to children. One may find: a story of a boy referred to as an orphan; a child killed by dangerous wiring in a street; a defiled seven-year-old girl who testified against a teacher at school; children in the street having run away from parental mistreatment, and a report on poems, songs and dances by primary school children to celebrate the Organisation of African Unity (OAU) decade for the survival, protection and development of the African Child.

The common theme running through these is the argument that children need protection – for being an orphan, from unsafe physical conditions, from parental mistreatment as well as life on the streets, for having been defiled – and the fact that an international tool such as an OAU declaration makes sense, and is made to make sense to children at a primary school level. These are important pointers to the principles and values that are being used and understood in the country at that particular time, and they suggest ways in which family tracing can be explained, made relevant, and related to the 'popular consciousness' of the time and place.

Decisions and dilemmas

Family tracing is fraught with social and cultural decisions and dilemmas which can only be addressed if there is a preparedness to talk about the principles and values on which it is based. In each programme, in each culture, questions have to be addressed such as: do adults always know best; which adults should decide what happens to children; should children be returned against their wishes; how do you choose between an inadequate institutional placement and a family placement in the context of acute shortages of food. There are no easy answers, and frank discussions of the values which guide decisions are essential.

LOGISTICS AND SYSTEMS

Logistics and systems are vital to family tracing. Designing and administering systems; preparing budgets; staffing and petrol vouchers; and organising tedious and extensive record keeping, are the practical foundation of family tracing. A mis-spelt name, or the wrong ordering of names, may mean the end of some child's hopes of reunification; inadequate staffing may mean the time can never be spent on finding a child's family.

Family tracing requires clearly defined job descriptions showing who is responsible for carrying out what; clear lines of accountability; clear agreements on funding, and on rights and responsibilities of both funders and receivers of funds.

Specialist or generalist tracing teams?

In practice one of the first decisions is whether to set up a tracing team whose job is mainly or only tracing, or whether to expect tracing to be carried out by staff who have other responsibilities such as social work, probation work or community work. Both methods require budgets to be drawn up, to include staff salaries (tracers, drivers, administrative staff) with an incentive system built into it (to ensure that children from far away places do have a chance of reunification); transport costs – sometimes four-wheel drive vehicles, motorcycles, or planes, spare tyres, insurance and more fuel than could possibly be imagined.

Effective record systems at all stages

Record systems are another essential ingredient. Without excellent record systems tracing cannot be done. Information from children has to be collected systematically, recorded rather than just remembered, analysed for clues. The success of tracing trips is closely related to the success of information-seeking and record keeping. Names are important: names of tribes, religions, clans, castes, parents' names, rivers, towns, schools, mountains. All help to suggest places to look and people to ask.

Ideally record keeping systems should be a priority at every stage of responding to an emergency: in camps, reception centres, orphanages. All too often they are not: they are seen as tasks which detract from the effort of feeding and sheltering children. They are not seen as ways of making exits easier, of ensuring there is a record of the past which helps many children return to it. Determined staff are needed to insist that these records are kept accurately, updated regularly and used intelligently.

The larger the tracing programme, the more important record keeping is. If a displacement is caused by a small specific problem, such as a very localised drought, flooding in an area, fighting near barracks, then both the problem and the solution is more manageable. If however the displacement covers large parts of a country, several millions of people, and possibly neighbouring countries as well, then training local people to set up and use a relevant type of record keeping system is a priority.

Simple and flexible systems

Clear guidelines for systems and record keeping are important, but they need to be both simple and flexible. They need to be simple because they are usually being used under very difficult circumstances which can include: little or untrained staff; semi-literate or non-literate volunteer/community workers; no agreement about the spelling of family names; little or no electricity for computers; telephone connections intermittent or non-existent and so on. But they also need to be flexible: the less confident people are about filling in forms, the easier it has to be made for them. It may be best that records are kept orally, using story-telling skills, until they can be communicated to someone who has paper, pens, forms and writing skills.

RECORD KEEPING: AN EXAMPLE

A good example of the need for relevant and efficient systems of record keeping emerged in the attempted repatriation and reintegration of Mozambican refugees from the asylum countries of Malawi, Tanzania, Swaziland, South Africa, Zambia and Zimbabwe. Within Mozambique a variety of forms and methods were being used in the tracing programme; to this was added the variety of forms and methods used – or designed but not used – in the various countries of asylum. It was argued that tracing should be seen as part of UNHCR's international protection and assistance function, but in practice it was a plethora of organisations setting up various attempts to trace, reunify or otherwise plan for unaccompanied children.

An action plan was drawn up, which included the following:
- strengthening and expanding the Mozambican tracing network;
- establishing systems of IDTR in each of the countries of asylum which are complementary to the system in Mozambique;
- preserving the principle of family unity during repatriation;
- sufficient training based on clear (and child-sensitive) guidelines to be conducted with field staff responsible not just for tracing, but also logistics and transport.

IS IT RELIEF OR DEVELOPMENT?

Is family tracing an emergency operation, part of a relief response? Partly yes, since most separations happen in emergencies and all the evidence suggests tracing needs to be done as quickly as possible, as soon after a separation as feasible. The later it is done the more difficult it is, and the higher the risk of non-reunification.

Or is family tracing a developmental operation, more concerned with the longer-term needs of children and their families? Partly yes, since much of the rationale behind family tracing is that children need to grow up in families, in their own communities, and there are many parts of socialisation which can only take place there. And communities need their children, as the young generation increasingly shares the responsibilities of making households and communities strong and successful.

How did it start? In some countries there is a tradition of children's institutions, but they are only able to offer minimal help. In these countries, tracing was a conscious step away from previous responses to children in need. It involved undoing, unlearning, rethinking responses. Often the practicalities of looking after large numbers of children contributed to the rethinking of policies.

In most countries however, tracing grew out of the dissolution of emergency responses – feeding camps, transit camps, refugee camps. The push factors were unrelated to children: political and administrative agreement had been reached that these emergency responses were no longer necessary and the next step was to close them, to withdraw funds, to move elsewhere. In practice, this has been the origin of many tracing programmes. It is to the credit of administrators and community workers, that when faced with this order, they have tried, with varying degrees of success, to design programmes which took children's interests and long-term needs into account. Sometimes tracing programmes grew out of the optimism of the end of a war, a negotiated peace; but other times camp administrators have been told to cease feeding, and hunger would disperse the children. This is an example of where tracing is the bridge between relief and longer-term development.

A bridge between relief and development

Perhaps family tracing *is* best seen as a bridge between relief and development, with roots in both, and with challenges for both. But bridges are difficult to classify and this may mean that family tracing sometimes falls between the two. When people cannot feed themselves and when government and other agencies cannot supply enough food, then family tracing may be seen as an individualistic luxury. And when development is defined so narrowly that it must have quantifiable economic benefits for a region, then tracing again is an irrelevant activity.

Both its strength and its weakness is that tracing is a bridging process, a movement of children, in time and in space.

IDENTIFICATION

CHILDREN SPEAK FOR THEMSELVES

Little has been written by children themselves on separation and its effects on them: written by a Ugandan boy in an orphanage, this poem is one of the exceptions. Two images come across very clearly: how separation is associated with something stopping what we might call growth, development, maturation; and of the future, and the uncertainty associated with 'tomorrow'.

Those children of prey,
Those angels who have lost their way,
Those disadvantaged, and always lonely,
Those afraid and always hungry.

A jewel lost in illusions
A treasure buried in confusion
A painter with no masterpiece
A necklace without a bead.

The child whose candle has stopped burning
The choir of singers has stopped singing
The delicate cloth has been torn
The silver slipper has been worn.

We children of fortune squander
What about the child with no mother
What of the child who is filled with fear
Who will dry her tears?

They are the children of tomorrow
But still their tears are full of sorrow
And today they are taking a stand
They are working hand in hand
Maybe we will never understand
Why orphans love this land.

Through all the hills and mountains
Through the rivers and water fountains
The orphans will hunger for love
But the love is only in heaven above

Who will save these children of distress
Who will unburden all their stress?

Ssentale Arthur
Massajja Boys Project
Kampala, Uganda

HOW DO CHILDREN BECOME SEPARATED?

Some of the ways children get separated include:
- Children are lost while fleeing from attacks on villages.
- Children may be lost when whole families or villages are on the move – looking for safety or food.
- Children are lost or attacked while searching for food.
- Children may be abducted by soldiers.
- Children may be lost during registration at camps or shelters.
- Children may be separated for special feeding at camps.
- Parents may die while travelling or fleeing.
- Parents may abandon children because either the parent or the child is thought too weak to carry on.
- Parents may leave a child at a hospital or camp, believing its chances of survival are better if left.

WHAT IS IDENTIFICATION?

This section looks at the 'identification' of separated children, children with tracing needs, which is the first step of the tracing sequence. Identification means little more than making a list of children who need tracing help – but this list should result from the drawing up and application, at regular intervals, of clear and comprehensive procedures for identifying children in different locations and children at different degrees of risk. When wars or displacements are ongoing, the identification of children needs to be active, pro-active, and based on the initiative of tracing teams.

Three questions are addressed:
- first, who should carry out this identification;
- second, how should identification take place; and
- third, where are the children likely to be who need identification and tracing help?

Although conceptually separate, identification often overlaps with documentation in practice and the two sections should be read together.

WHO SHOULD DO THE IDENTIFICATION?

> *Children cannot be expected to ask for tracing:*
> *they must be offered it.*

Who should be responsible for the first step in tracing: the identification of children who need tracing help? There are two main ways of setting up tracing systems: using specialist staff or giving new responsibilities to existing staff. Each has advantages and disadvantages, and in every situation these need to be weighed up before decisions are made.

Specialist teams

A specialist team may be more effective in the short term: they can be trained intensively and they acquire experience intensively too. They can be recruited for skills such as lateral thinking (important in tracing with only fragmented information) and skills in communicating with children (important in documentation and reunification). They have few competing responsibilities and their pay can be made conditional on certain standards and conditions being met – such as travelling extensively. They can become a pioneering team of dedicated idealists with a high success rate.

But a specialist team may be in competition with general social/community workers – for status, recognition or pay. They may attract more of all of those rewards from international donors, thereby creating resentment and ill-will. They will need to be disbanded when the tracing is completed or the budget exhausted, and their skills will be lost. From the point of view of the country, or its government, a specialist tracing team is not good long-term investment. It does not add to the skilled infrastructure left behind when the emergency has receded.

New responsibilities for existing teams

Generic social workers, community workers, district officers or teachers can also be trained to carry out tracing, as part of their other work. The advantages are that tracing then becomes absorbed as a part of work in the community – it is not an 'external' activity, clearly identified with international donors. The children are not singled out, are less stigmatised and also less privileged. Tracing becomes part of a range of other work routinely done in the community by people in and of the community. Skills learnt stay in the community and the people doing the tracing and the reunification may also be the same people monitoring and following up.

But this general model is much less likely to work if large numbers of separated children are involved. The workload becomes too heavy and tracing is likely to be a low priority task. But even when the numbers are not large, there are other problems: learning through limited experience is slow, the pre-requisite abilities may not be there in the first place; and competing demands may be high. In practice, the general model has often required a system of incentives to make it work: a per reunification fee or per diem for travel. But even these do not always ensure that children from remote areas are reunified. And a system which rewards reunification without monitoring whether what is done is in the best interest of the child, also has its dangers.

Combining the two

In many situations a combination of these two systems emerges. A specialist tracing team may be set up, which decides the methodology: designs·forms, sets up systems, travels widely. They may just start the tracing programme – or they may do the bulk of tracing needed after a specific emergency. They then move into a training role and hand over responsibility to district level staff. At that stage efficiency often falls dramatically and accountability issues have to be built into the programme.

Membership of tracing teams

Where should the membership of tracing teams be drawn from?
- International NGOs have certain strengths: they can usually access funds and may also be good at planning.
- National Ministry staff also have important strengths: they open doors to enable new initiatives to get off the ground; they legitimise programmes; they also plan and coordinate services to areas and peoples.

- Local staff are essential because they know the area, the language, the customs, the culture.

The question then is not which of these should develop the tracing programme but how they should work in partnership. NGOs are often useful in order to launch a programme and draw attention to the issue. An initial plan may well come from them. A good partnership with government requires spelling out clearly what each is going to provide and what each can expect. NGOs and national governments work best where there is a clear code of guidance and ethics and where the two meet frequently to discuss and review needs and developments. Local staff need to be involved at an early stage, and high standards need to be expected and rewarded. A good partnership is not easy to achieve and needs a lot of work.

COOPERATION BETWEEN SPECIALIST TRACING TEAMS AND COMMUNITY LEADERS: A PERSONAL ACCOUNT

A specialist team worker gave the following account of cooperation with local leaders. The local community was the key to success.

"We started working at orphanages and at centres for street children: we used to go regularly to both. Then we started going out to the districts and organising community meetings. At first we did everything: identifying the children, interviewing them, moving them, placing them, tracing their families, then moving them again. But we learnt to involve the community in the whole process: in the documentation, in putting posters up, asking them to tell us if they knew these families. We started working closely with the community to identify substitute families as well as families who had lost a child. We recorded details and cross-referenced all information.

When we go to the districts we ask the community leaders to organise the meetings – meetings specially about separated children. If political people want to come, we ask them not to wear uniform. We as tracing workers chair the meetings, but the community leaders sit with us and talk to the people. Otherwise people are afraid. Too much has happened for them to trust easily. Now they only feel safe with their own people. People in this area were afraid of children being stolen – first by the guerrillas, and then by the government. It has happened. So we tell them: 'We are not going to take the children away. If we find the families, then we will send a message to your community leader and maybe the family themselves will come. Then you can talk about the best interest of the child.' Gradually we won their confidence. Now they come to us and inform us: 'These children arrived yesterday; they will stay with us; you find their family'."

WHERE TO LOOK FOR CHILDREN

Identification needs to start with a planning session to draw up a list of places where separated children might be. This list needs to be drawn up for both urban and rural areas, with people who have local knowledge.

Visible and invisible children

Some unaccompanied children will be living in places where they are clearly identifiable as unaccompanied children needing help: these are the visible children. But many others will not. They may be part of the hidden numbers of children who, although they are lost, are not visibly lost. They simply merge into the surrounding households, institutions, environment and streets: these are the invisible children.

If one is trying to close a feeding centre or refugee camp, then children are relatively easily identifiable. But in most war situations, there are many more children who need help than those already registered and grouped in one clearly designated place. And where tracing is taken up as national policy, where a government decides that every child should have the chance of growing up with his or her family, then the identification of children must move from the rather reactive documentation of children already identified in a relief response, to the much more active search for the invisible children who also need tracing help.

Children already identified as unaccompanied and housed and cared for separately – perhaps in orphanages or children's feeding programmes – are the obvious starting point of any identification process. Children who are registered as part of households – either in camps or out of them – when they are not in fact related to the families of the household, are likely to be the numerically much larger group, whose invisibility may make them more vulnerable to abuse or neglect. Reaching this second group requires a great deal of education and preparation of the displaced community.

In many wars and disaster situations people are reluctant to give detailed personal information because it may be dangerous. People are afraid. What will be done with the names of the children? Will they be abruptly removed? Will the new leaders take them as theirs to do what they wish? And in some situations an extra child means an extra ration card and the fear of having that ration card taken away leads to silence.

Identification and a national education programme

Identification requires a national education programme to address these fears. Before any attempt is made to locate such invisible children, tracing needs to be explained in theory and in practice. Explanations have to be given as to how tracing fits in with national reconstruction, the reconstruction of families and communities. Explanations need to show the benefits of tracing to children and families and how it will not harm those who have helped children by sheltering them. Explanations need to be given as to whether children will stay with the unrelated households until families are traced and what will happen if children do not wish to go and live with their families. Local communities will only participate if they understand and trust a tracing programme.

A national education programme on tracing should be developed with the help of all possible forms of media. Newspaper articles and radio programmes and television pictures and leaflets and talks to community leaders, political leaders, traditional leaders, all help. Television is the most restricted since it reaches so few people; yet it has such visual impact if children are portrayed and it is a good educator. Newspapers tend to take a long time to reach remote places – but often have a wide and repeated readership. Community leaders are often the key to encouraging a community to take part in a registration process – and they need to be addressed early, before they speak out against tracing.

A NATIONAL EDUCATION PROGRAMME

Use as many of these media tools as possible:
- Newspaper articles
- Newspaper editorials
- Radio programmes
- Newspaper pictures of reunification
- TV programmes
- Talks to community leaders
- Leaflets

Key issues:
- Popular political leaders associated with the programme
- Traditional leaders involved and speaking out for the programme
- Pictures and testimonies of reunified children

Keep the message simple:
- Explaining why tracing is being done
- Convey that tracing is safe
- Explain how families themselves can trace

Children in refugee camps/displaced camps/transit camps

Children in camps should be registered as soon as possible. Ideally this should be done when they first arrive, and done thoroughly to include interviews with the people bringing them in.

Identification should start with all children without any adult to look after them, moving on subsequently to other children. This usually involves volunteers going through camps systematically talking to each head of household as well as the community leaders. A register needs to be prepared of all households where such children live, for later interviewing.

Children in orphanages/children's homes

Children should be identified as soon as they arrive or very soon thereafter.

Children in police stations

An effective tracing system requires training of local and national police together with regular visits to police stations to monitor police actions in relation to unaccompanied children.

Many unaccompanied children in urban areas pass through the hands of police at some stage. In many countries there is little coordination between ministries of social welfare (or their equivalent) and the police. Good practice would mean police liaising closely with the department, handing children over to them as soon as possible; interviewing and carrying out documentation themselves and becoming active partners in a tracing programme.

Bad practice frequently means police are ignorant of the need for tracing and the importance of early documentation; they are slow to liaise, coordinate and plan for the welfare of the child; they may be involved in attempting to elicit a bribe for freeing the child; or they may be more heavily involved in perpetrating some form of abuse – beating the children, using them as cheap labour or for sexual purposes.

Children in hospitals

During wars and population displacements many children end up in hospital alone because of physical injury, often combined with malnutrition, nervous exhaustion and trauma. They may have been brought in by soldiers, neighbours, strangers. All paediatric and casualty child admissions who have no visitors in the first three days should go on an 'at risk of being unaccompanied' register (part of the national tracing programme). Early responses to such separation may prevent much longer periods of separation.

Another group of children in hospital also need to be documented: young children who come into hospital with their mother because she herself is sick. If the mother dies, the child is left alone. When these children are then removed from the hospitals, it is important that the mother's records accompany the child, and tracing begins as soon as possible, with the aim of establishing whether the child can be placed back in the community with a female relative immediately or at a later date when it is weaned.

Registration of children in the community

It is common when large numbers of families flee or are resettled that they will find unaccompanied children en route and many will absorb them into their households. While wars continue, reunification may not be possible or easy; but early identification allows information to be collected which makes later reunification easier.

This process requires publicity and education of the community. This must be done in the various languages that are used and must have leaders – political, administrative, religious, community – showing their support. Minority groups – religious, ethnic, caste, tribal, language – need particular reassurance: they may fear that the majority group may be taking away minority group children to harm them.

Households who have 'taken in' an unaccompanied child should be encouraged to *register* the child as soon as possible. A registration point needs to be set up, preferably at a neutral and safe location such as a community location or local church, temple or mosque, and not a political location. Teachers can also be encouraged to help to identify separated children.

Registration systems need to ensure that there are no negative conse-quences – such as encouraging families to abandon children they have cared for. Nor should families be encouraged to register children simply as a means of getting economic benefits.

Children in soldiers' camps

It is common in wars for children to be picked up by all sides of the fighting. Sometimes they are picked up for their own protection. Often they may be used as porters to carry food; as cooks, cleaners, messengers and as sexual partners; and of course also as fighters. Boy soldiers and girl soldiers are increasingly being used in wars as frontline fighters. As part of any demobilisation or negotiated peace settlement, it is important to include these children in identification programmes.

Street children

With and without wars, children end up on the streets of many cities. Identification of street children should be a part of all national tracing programmes. Some street children may be very happy to be reunified where their separation was involuntary. Others may have separated voluntarily from extreme poverty or violence, and for these the primary aim of identification and documentation would still be to plan for their future, but not necessarily for their return. Gaining the trust of street children is important before any identification or documentation can take place.

PRIORITISING WHERE TO LOOK

When a list of places where separated children might be has been drawn up, the next step is to prioritise these places in terms of need. Where are the children most vulnerable, where are they most at risk? Identification should be planned: where will it start, and when and where will it move to next? It needs to spell out explicitly which children are most at risk and least at risk and which can wait longer. This will be determined by local conditions – in the community, in police cells, in army camps, in orphanages, as well as the number of children at risk, the size of budgets and so on.

ABUSE

Some children have run away or been separated from families where they have suffered various kinds of abuse. The 'best interest' of the child always requires an assessment, a judgment about what is best.

Abuse may be physical, emotional or sexual, and may include passive neglect. Typical examples of above are:
- children whose parents drink too much and beat them excessively
- children being badly mistreated by stepparents
- children constantly and severely beaten by their parents
- children born to prostitutes and left in an unsafe environment
- children forced into habitual stealing of food and money for survival
- children forced into excessive labour or trade, including prostitution
- children forced to flee because relatives want to kill them for their land

Examples of abuse from hospital reports*

- rape – by soldiers
- burning – by parents
- assaults – by parents and relatives
- poisoning – parents and relatives
- grievous harm – parents
- battered children – unknown perpetrators
- homicide – not known
- defilement – not stated

Two things are important:
- First, to gain the trust of the child so that they can talk about the abuse. Otherwise reunification may place the child in renewed danger.
- Second, to assess whether the abuse can be addressed and further abuse prevented – perhaps by the involvement of local community leaders. If not, then an alternative will be needed.

---

* Paper by Hon Justice Mukasa-Kikonyogo, Judge of the High Court of Uganda, 1990 for Child Law Review Committee. Report on the Proceedings of the Child Law Review Committee Workshop, Sept 1990, set up by Minister of Relief and Social Rehabilitation. Uganda.

CHILD TRAUMA

Trauma describes the response of both children and adults to difficult and disturbing situations: it may be expressed in many different ways – shock, denial, anger and aggression. Much has been written about the importance of recognising children suffering from trauma, and how to respond to it. However, little has been done in practice. Perhaps because, in conditions of wars and displacements, so many children are affected, and so many adults who in theory should be providing the diagnosis and the care are also affected, it is difficult to give it the priority that it needs.

In terms of priorities for identification of unaccompanied children, awareness of the effects of trauma are important at three stages:

- When choosing which children are most in need of help, their level of distress is an important element. If the short-term care situation is such that the experience of trauma can be addressed – for example by special play and dance and discussion programmes in camps, where children can start to come to terms with their experiences – then this should not be disrupted. In one country six months' time was allocated for this 'healing process' in transit camps for boy soldiers. Often it is more effective to address it in the community that children have been returned to. The help of elders, community leaders and school teachers may be invaluable.

- Documentation of children who are traumatised often takes longer, is more difficult, and there are more emotional obstacles to remembering and talking about what happened in the past. This should be allowed for in allocating time spent with each child, and a fixed time allocation per child should not be the model used.

- The third stage relates to preparation of children and families for reunification. This is dealt with later.

WAYS OF RESPONDING TO TRAUMA: AN EXAMPLE

The UNHCR Guidelines for Refugee Children describe ways of working with children through leaders from the local community. They get the children involved in story-telling, drawing, dance, playing with clay or drama. All the activities have to be cultur-ally based, not externally imposed, and the aim is to allow children to express and listen to feelings and community responses putting the war and the atrocities in per-spective. The aim of the activities is to give meaning to the past; to enable the children to disassociate themselves from the guilt, yet to start healing again.

Save the Children (US) has developed a programme in Malawi where Mozambican war affected children act out games and stories from their experiences. For example, one popular game is where children have to escape from others holding them. The programme seems to have contributed to the children's healing in commu-nity-based group settings. The programme faced problems of stigmatising children and being labelled as a programme for 'mad' children. Both these problems have been addressed, by joint programmes with non-traumatised children and by more involvement of community leaders, parents and traditional healers.

Save the Children (UK) has produced a manual in this series for people working with children in difficult situations (see Appendix 2).

Recovering from trauma

Much healing happens by itself, but it can be helped to happen.

Research in Malawi concluded that:

- Some of the problems appeared to result from exposure to specific traumas and the children needed help to come to terms with them.
- Other problems seemed to result from the children's efforts to cope in a situation where violence was the norm. Many of the attitudes, values and behaviours the children needed to survive being kidnapped became inappropriate when they were freed.
- Children's efforts to re-adjust after their dehumanising experiences were facilitated primarily through their relationships with their new caretakers/families. In the final analysis, it was the ability of the women to with-stand the children's initial aggression that enabled them to begin to re-establish trust in people.

CHECKLIST: identification of children for tracing

- Weigh up the advantages and disadvantages of specialist and generalist teams.

- Draw together all the evidence on visible and invisible separated children.

- Identify the obstacles to children and carers revealing the existence of separated children. Decide how to address these.

- Launch a national education campaign about the importance of tracing generally.

- Specify what households caring for separated children should do.

- Specify what families searching for their children should do.

- Make a list of all the places where separated children may be and rank them in terms of the vulnerability of their situation.

- From the above draw together a plan of where documenting children will start.

DOCUMENTATION

PERSONAL STATEMENTS OF TRACING STAFF

"I find documenting children very rewarding. If you approach them well and gain their confidence, then they will talk."

"Sometimes it's easy. But sometimes it's difficult. Some children don't want to talk to you. Some have been separated so long they can't remember details. Some have had difficulties with their families and do not want to talk to you about them. Some are traumatised and do not want to remember what happened to them. Street children are also very difficult – they don't want to talk."

"Some of my staff are very good. They get the children to tell them their story, like the grandparents told them stories. They don't ask too many formal questions."

WHAT IS DOCUMENTATION?

Documentation is essentially a combination of child-sensitive practices and efficient logistics and systems. This section looks at some of the child-sensitive practices involved in the documentation of children, and at designing a system for documentation – with lots of forms!

The essence of documentation is twofold: first, having staff who have skills with children: listening, communicating, giving them time, reassuring, helping them to come to terms with the past – as well as eliciting information from them; and second, a system of documentation which has ways of recording this information, and procedures for getting the information to the right places. In some ways these are polar opposite skills – one requires warmth and lateral thinking, the other meticulous concern for detail and procedures. A tracing programme cannot choose between them: it takes the marriage of the two to document successfully.

Documentation is a collection of facts about the past and the present; but it is also an assessment about the present and the future. It is a social history but it is also a tool for choosing which relative to seek and how to try and plan the future life of the child.

THE AIMS OF DOCUMENTATION

In order to acquire comprehensive and comparable information, the aims of documentation must be clear to everyone. Documentation has three goals:
- to get as much information about the past as possible to enable a successful tracing to take place;
- to get a good picture of the present situation of the child in order to establish whether any immediate intervention is necessary; and
- to develop a picture of what the child would like for the future.

THE IMPORTANCE OF LISTENING

The essence of documenting is first, listening to children and, second, recording what they say. This sounds like it should be easy, yet it is often one of the most difficult parts of tracing. There are many obstacles which stand in the way of adults listening to and hearing children.

Obstacles to listening

Some adults think that children should listen to adults and adults do not need to listen to children. This attitude may be deeply ingrained, making it difficult for adults to encourage children to talk to them and share their often difficult experiences.

Sometimes adults do not make the time to listen to children. When children cannot give accurate fast and factual answers to questions on a form, adults sometimes stop talking to them and turn to the nearest adult for information instead. Children's sense of time is also often different from adults and needs some probing.

Obstacles to hearing

Separated children have inevitably been through a difficult time and this means sometimes they find it difficult to talk about the past. Some adults interpret the resulting hesitancy as not knowing and move on to the next question or stop trying.

Sometimes adults get upset by hearing the children's painful pasts and they stop children from telling them more.

Obstacles to understanding

Sometimes adults are too concerned with completing forms and not concerned enough with understanding the events as seen by the child. They may ask their questions too fast and too mechanically, not allowing the child to tell their story their way. They may dismiss the details that are important to the child. They may not be able to understand that what seems important to the child may be different from what seems important to an adult.

Obstacles to allowing children to voice their choices

In many cultures children are seen as their families' responsibility, and in this context, it is the family who assumes the responsibility for making choices. The concept of children exercising individual choices independently of their families is often unheard of. But by definition the context has changed and no longer applies for separated children: the family is not there for them to decide what may be best for the child. This changed situation is often not taken into account when the idea that children could contribute to decisions about their future is being dismissed.

PREPARATION

Communities where children live need to be prepared for the documentation and children themselves need to be prepared as well. Explanations are important, and both adults and children need time to absorb them.

Resistance to documentation is frequent. In orphanages and refugee camps, care staff often feel threatened by the arrival of tracing teams. There may be strong bonds between at least some of the children and the care staff. There are usually strong bonds between the children themselves. There is concern that tracing staff may not want what is best for the children, and that they may be sending them to unsafe and poor areas which would not be in the best interests of the children they have cared for. Furthermore, if the children are all reunited with their families, the care staff will be out of work. Together these two fears are powerful forces of resistance to successful documentation. They may influence children directly or directly, communicating to them the dangers of talking to strangers and opening up past wounds.

Substitute families may also resist documentation if they are not well prepared. Why should they allow the children in their care to talk freely to people they do not know but who seem to be powerful enough to make seemingly arbitrary decisions about whether a child stays or goes, and can send them off into unknown situations with no protection?

If adults have to facilitate access to children, children nevertheless must be willing to talk. Many are only too happy to do so – they have not had much opportunity of individual adult attention and interest and it can be a very rewarding experience. Many children open up like flowers and talk in a very natural and honest way. Others do not, and need a great deal of reassurance.

DOCUMENTATION INTERVIEWING

A safe environment

The documentation interviewing should take place where the children feel comfortable and where there is privacy. If possible it should not be in an office. Sitting in the garden; walking around the plot to examine the crops or the vegetables; or sitting in private in one of the rooms of the house where other people can neither interrupt nor hear is preferable. Privacy is important; unhurried time is important, as is an unhurried manner.

FRIGHTENED CHILDREN

Most children are afraid of change and many get used to their new families. It's not that they don't want their own family, they just do not want another disruption, another change. Especially the little ones.

Many of the older ones are afraid of going home because they remember what the soldiers/guerrillas did and they are afraid that it is still continuing.

Others were forced to take part in killings or in other war activities and they are afraid how their community and their families will respond. They are afraid to risk another separation, this time based on rejection.

Many children feel guilty and ashamed. It may be simply guilt about having survived, especially if they know that others members of their family did not.

Or it may be guilt and shame about having failed to protect someone. Often when fleeing children lose their younger brothers and sisters. They then feel their families and communities will hold them responsible for the life of the younger child.

Dealing with children's anxieties

The interview should have been explained to the child in the presence of adults; it now needs to be explained again. It is wrong to raise hopes too high and promise reunification and equally it is wrong to frighten the child with instant removal. Even when children really do want to be with their families, returning home may be frightening.

Sometimes 'going home' is associated with the dangers of what happened before. Change is often frightening to children and choosing another disruption and displacement may be too much. Other children might be afraid to hear of the deaths of their family and having their fears confirmed may be what makes them afraid. Others still are trapped in feelings of guilt – perhaps for not having been able to prevent the death or loss of a younger sister or brother, or for having escaped the death that others could not. Still others may feel angry with their parents for not protecting them – from being beaten, raped, abducted. All these complex emotions are present in the documentation interview, and interviewing staff must know how to interpret them, address them, comfort the children, and at the same time to get factual information from them.

These emotions are normal and widespread and are part of working with separated children. But there are even more damaged children, frequently referred to as traumatised children, who need a lot of time, patience and stability before they can talk. In all countries there are some children who turn temporarily blind or mute, children who have separated themselves from their painful experiences by extreme forms of survival strategies. Documentation must go hand in hand with a programme of healing.

Juan was an eight-year-old who could talk, but could not tell you what had happened to him. His mouth formed the words but no voice came out. He was described as very agitated and very traumatised. He was placed in an orphanage. In his case documentation took four years. That is when he felt safe enough to talk about how his parents were killed and what he was forced to do. Two elder brothers were eventually traced.

The documentation should proceed at the child's pace – slowly if they are young, gradually covering more and more ground. Some children are very sure their parents are dead, because the finality is easier to accept than the uncertainty. Questions must be asked about why they think the parents are dead. Children must also be given the opportunity to voice their choice about where they may wish to live or which relative should be sought first. This is an essential part of the documentation. At the end it is important to discuss options with the child, agree a plan and explain to the child what will happen. This explanation should include a realistic timetable of what will happen when, and some reassurance about keeping them informed of progress. At the end of the documentation the child should feel that someone is seriously planning for their future.

Length of interviews

Ideally, it is the child who should determine how long the documentation interview lasts. Where a child is mature, old enough to understand, talks easily, can identify their parents' name and their village, needs no current intervention and has clear views on wanting to return to her parents, the documentation process can probably be done in one interview and it could take as little as forty-five minutes, yet still be done thoroughly.

At the other extreme, where a child is very disturbed and very closed and where she does not want or is unable to communicate, documentation can take weeks or months to do. It might mean establishing a relationship with the child through play, taking a special interest in the child, devoting a small piece of time to her every day, encouraging the child to express herself through drawings, songs, playing with dolls, telling stories – as well as asking direct questions.

Who should interview the children?

Generally there are two ways of doing documentation interviews: existing care staff can do them on a routine basis or specialist teams can arrive and interview separated children. Each method has advantages and disadvantages.

Existing care staff are less threatening to children since the children know them; they are in a good position to do gradual documentation, adding bits of information to the picture as they emerge and not needing to get it all in one piece of allotted time; the views of the care staff may also be shared and the final assessment of needs may be a fuller one. However, care staff may have low or no educational qualifications which makes recording information difficult; they may have little understanding of tracing where children are unable to communicate the relevant information; they may be too busy keeping orphanages or camps going with little budgets, food or firewood and they may have vested interests in not reunifying children.

Specialist teams may be more efficient – they may be well trained with lots of experience in documentation; they may use their experience of tracing to know what kind of information is useful when one is searching for villages with no names and for parents who have been displaced.

But teams have limited time and most cannot spend a long time with individuals building relationships and breaking down resistance. They may be good with the easy children, they may be less good with the silent ones. This is, however, not necessarily the case – in one case, organising football matches was the way tracing teams relaxed children and became accepted in a camp very quickly. They observed who chose whom for which side of the game and who cheered whom – all useful information in the categorisation of children by region and tribe.

Increasingly, tracing programmes are turning to community leaders to undertake the documentation at least of children in the rural community. This is partly because it saves the expense of tracing staff travelling for days to talk to a child for an hour or so; but it is also because community leaders have some of the strengths of each side: they have more time to establish a relationship; they do not usually have vested interests in maintaining an existing living arrangement; and they can play a useful monitoring role, overseeing the child's placement while tracing attempts are undertaken.

DILEMMAS OF DOCUMENTATION: TARGETING

Several hundred people escaped from guerrilla bases, arrived hungry and frightened with no food or possessions. The children had large bellies, the babies had sores all over. They were sitting among the flies despondently. Then the landrover arrived and hope filled people's eyes. They crowded around the man who got out. They did not understand the meaning of his words, why he was looking for separated children.

One mother asked, very softly, if he had milk for her twins. She had none and they were dying. He sent her away. Others came and brought their own problems: illness, hunger and more hunger. Eventually they understood, he was only interested in children who were not here with their parents. They remained puzzled. Why was he interested in them?

Many were here with their nephews and nieces. What did he want with them? He talked some more. Eventually someone remembered the name of a child with no family there. She was sent for.

Even before she arrived, the authoritarian young man barked questions about her. Name? Date of birth? Parents' name? The girl was found and pushed to the centre of the crowd where she stood silently, afraid, head bowed, eyes looking down. Everyone looked on, with resentment. Was she going to get food, she alone of all these hungry people? But no, the man just wrote down the details and then his driver drove him away.

RECORDING THE RESULTS OF THE INTERVIEWS

> *No child has dropped from the skies.*
> *No child has no one.*

Getting the information from children is the first part of documentation; recording it in a way that is useful at a later time and in a later place, to people who have not spoken to the child, is the second part of the process of documentation.

A variety of forms, filing systems and small bureaucracies have been set up in each country for this. Each country tends to have its own system and procedures – and often cannot conceive that there is any other way of doing it. In some countries several systems co-exist, to the frustration of the local people and because of the obstinacy of the different organisations managing the tracing.

Designing recording forms

- Forms need to be short and simple. They may be used by people who can barely read or write; by people standing in the scorching sun, without even a book to rest on let alone a desk to sit at; by people surrounded by crowds pushing and shoving and in a language that is often neither people's first nor second.
- Forms need to be comprehensive. This means they cannot be restricted to a very structured form where ticks in boxes are sufficient. The complexities of situations have to be captured, since there is often no second opportunity to return to ask an additional question. Examples of forms are given in Appendix 1.

Key questions

The key questions depend on the situation in the country. Some tracing systems depend on tracing teams going out to find families; others depend more on families reporting children they are looking for; still others depend largely on the recognition of photographs. For each system there will be different key questions. However, the essence of all questions is the understanding of the past and the present, regardless of local circumstances. Questions are about:

- **The child.** The name of the child, age, language, clan/tribe/religion/caste.
- **The family.** The names of the family members she was living with – all siblings (with ages), parents, grandparents, uncles, aunts – the larger the number of relatives known the better the chance of finding one of them. If any are employed or with a recognised position in the village that is useful too. For each, whether 'dead' or 'don't know' .
- **The past.** Where was she living when she became separated. If she cannot give the name of the village, then ask questions about the area: any mountains or rivers or market towns, and what are their names? Any churches, mosques, temples; the names of schools, teachers, or community leaders.
- **Separation.** A description of the separating event. The detail may help identify where it was. For example, who attacked the village, what were they wearing, what were they saying, which way did you run and which way did the others run etc. If it was recent, what was the child wearing, who was with her etc.
- **The present.** What has happened to her since, how did she get where she is now, how is she treated, how appropriate is it for her to stay where she is, what are her short-term needs and wishes?
- **The future.** What are her long-term wishes? If children feel safe enough to talk and have formed some kind of trusting relationship with the person doing the documentation, many will identify at this stage which relative they would prefer to live with, if they were found. This is particularly important if all the nearest relatives are dead: it is children in these situations who are in greatest danger of neglect or abuse if their reunifications do not consider the children's own wishes.

An administrative system for the forms

There are many ways of formulating a system for the completed documentation forms to reach the places they are meant to. One method is to do three copies of the form, leave one at district level (or at the children's home), send one to provincial level and one to the capital, to the national Ministry of Welfare – or to whichever Ministry assumes responsibility for the tracing programme. But this is only the start of the system. It may be useful to have additional forms for some or all of the following:

- forms for parents to register their lost children;
- forms for tracers to record what attempts at tracing they have made with what outcomes;

- forms to verify the details the family gave of the child they are claiming to be related to;
- forms for use during the reunification itself, when the family receiving the child agree and sign in front of community leaders who act as witnesses, that they will look after the child.

In addition, an effective system involves the following stages:

- designing and piloting forms to see if they work;
- printing enough for a national programme (if that is what is being attempted);
- distributing them in such a way that they are at the right place at the right time;
- training staff to understand them, be motivated about using them and be able to use them effectively;
- (possibly) handing out lists of towns and villages together with a map of the country, to facilitate location and accurate spelling;
- setting up a system for them to be re-ordered before they run out and lead to the cessation of tracing because the forms are out of stock;
- periodically reviewing them to see if any changes need to be incorporated.

PHOTOGRAPHS

Some countries have highly developed tracing systems, and have traced several thousands of children without a camera or a single photograph. These systems rely on tracers to do the tracing and to use the verbal information rather than the visual information, to try and locate family members. This system can of course only work in countries where travel is possible. Other countries rely on cameras and photographs to play a part in tracing. In some of these countries the photographs are an additional tool for tracing, in others they are the main or even only tool.

Where, for example, travel is nearly impossible, perhaps because a civil war is raging and any 'official' staff, such as government tracing staff, are likely to be killed, then photographing children, creating posters of the various separated children, and sending these to the areas where families may be living, may be a useful method. It usually involves the following steps:

- Issuing documenting staff with cameras and with film – and with instructions on where to keep them for safety when they are not in use. Instant Polaroid films may be useful but are very expensive.

- Issuing instructions on how to take pictures: close to the child and in the sunlight; three or even four photographs may be necessary; and the name, age, location of the child and date of each photograph should be written on the back immediately. The pictures may be sent again to provincial and national level – and in some tracing systems the child herself has been given one – as a gift and a symbol of the tracing.
- If there are large numbers of children from a particular province or district, it may be efficient to produce a poster with 12 or 24 photographs printed on it, giving names and ages of the children. These need to be printed and distributed to the relevant area and can be displayed at clinics, hospitals, market places, churches – or anywhere public where large numbers of people pass it, see it and can discuss it. These posters must give instructions on what people should do if they know where the family is.

The risks of photographs

A documentation system relying heavily on photographs is often appealing since it seems to apply technology in a useful way. However, it has many risks and these need to be discussed and debated before the decision is made to use and/or rely on this method.

- First, there is the cost. It is very expensive to distribute cameras and films; orphanages and district offices often have them stolen; and they need frequent replacing if tracing is to continue.
- Second, there are security risks in relation to cameras in most wars, with soldiers and others shooting at the sight of cameras, assuming them to be weapons of information-gathering for the war.
- Third, there are cultural issues to explore. In some Muslim cultures people do not want themselves to be photographed – and fear the camera nearly as much as the gun. Others have no objection, but are unused to looking at pictures and find it difficult to recognise even children they know well in blurred two dimensional greyish photos – and hence they do not work well. In Ethiopia staff reported that even parents did not recognise photographs of their children; they looked too different.
- Fourth, they create a dependency within the tracing system. We observed several provinces and districts where tracing had stopped altogether, simply because there was no film. Films had become equated with tracing, and nothing could be done for separated children for six months or more because there was no money for films. In other

districts tracing was slow because there was a problem in paying for the posters to be printed: six months or more could easily elapse between a child being photographed and his poster even being printed. This is a long time for a child to be waiting unnecessarily.

- Fifth, there are, as always, unintended consequences for all the tools of tracing. We came across posters of separated children which had been acquired by individuals who, not understanding their purpose, used them to adorn the walls of their otherwise bare huts.

None of this means photographs should not be used. However, it seems important to avoid dependency on cameras by assessing the risks and trying to prevent the problems from the start.

COMPUTERS

Some of the arguments which apply to photographs also apply to computers. Many countries have run family tracing programmes with little more than a filing cabinet and this is perfectly feasible. However, computers have proved useful in many western projects, and there are advantages and disadvantages to their use in tracing too.

At best they can hold a great deal of information in one place; they can cross-refer names and locations; they can match up children found with children lost. They can be used for resource planning; for statistics in documentations and reunifications; for identifying brothers and sisters separated in the system; for identifying children with disabilities and what their needs are. Potentially, they can speed up much that is usually done manually – if it is done at all. Computer print-outs of children's names can be sent to provinces or districts – or even community leaders in villages. Families searching for their children can register these and a 'computer search' can follow. Using villages of origin as the key identifier helps planning the tracing.

But there are both ideological and practical problems. Ideologically, there is immediately the question of dependency. Do computers create another strand of dependency with national staff being unconfident, possibly needing expatriates to explain and maintain and update and develop systems? Furthermore, for many senior national government staff, priorities are not the location of separated children, but maybe the demobilisation of a couple of million soldiers or the return of a million refugees or the payment of the wages of the entire civil service with no money available. These may be seen as far more urgent issues, and many government staff, if given the choice, would choose a computer for these priorities and not for family tracing.

Then there are the practical issues. Electricity is sporadic. Names can be spelt in half a dozen ways, making alphabetical lists and cross-checking unreliable. In some cultures and areas dozens of children have the same names. In others children receive new names after initiation rights or simply have nick-names. Unlike people, computers have no imagination and are not good at lateral thinking. In villages and even some districts there may not be anyone confident either to receive or analyse print-outs. They can be stolen. And again, in wars, creating lists of people may be dangerous – they may be used to identify children who can be kidnapped for fighting, or for identifying families who are from the 'wrong' areas, religions or tribal groups and who become targets for killing.

DOCUMENTATION IN INSTITUTIONS

Documenting children in institutions has its own set of problems. First, historically, most institutions have not systematically documented children who have come to them. Children have often lived in orphanages for years without there being a casefile on the child, a record of the circumstances of their arrival, a record of who and where the family is, or a plan for their future. Yet these are all good practice, and their absence makes attempts at documentation years later very difficult. The child needs to be interviewed carefully, and so do older children and staff who were in the home at the time when the child was admitted. Documentation should take place immediately when a child is received, even if there is no immediate hope of tracing the family.

Second, there are institutional obstacles to documentation in many orphanages. Some staff are very attached to the children and have close relationships with them. Just as children fear change, many staff do as well. Documentation of children in 'their' children's homes may mean a number of things. It may upset many children, leading to tears, to aggression, to bedwetting. It may mean the children remain unsettled for a long time, expecting either to be moved and reunited immediately, or to have their worst fears of the deaths of their families confirmed. It may mean some children are moved fairly soon while others remain, increasingly upset and uncertain. In the long run, it may mean the closure of the home and the loss of their jobs.

Sometimes staff act to obstruct documentation of children. They may frighten the children so they choose not to talk. They may threaten the children if they do talk. They may teach them how to lie and to say that they saw all their families killed or that they came from a part of the country where no family member will ever be traced. Some staff simply do not allow tracing.

For both staff and children reunification involves a new separation which is not always easy. Adolescent children value their peer groups and their educational opportunities and these together may be important reasons for resisting documentation.

Sometimes the problems are more practical. There are not enough resources for tracing: no paper, pens, or transport. When a child comes in, documentation and tracing should be immediate – because the chances of success are highest then. But where both the motivation and the money are lacking, tracing is often delayed.

DOCUMENTATION AND SHORT-TERM PLACEMENT NEEDS

Having documented what the child's tracing needs are, it remains important to ask whether it is in the child's best interests to stay where they are or whether they should be moved, while tracing is progressing. If the living situation seems safe and the child does not wish to be removed, then generally the fewer moves the child has to make the better. A common mistake in past tracing programmes has been to move children and group children in various waiting camps for the convenience of staff and easy access. Children's need for stability and predictability has often been ignored. Good practice generally means allowing children to choose and encouraging the stability of the same environment and the continuation of routines. Where this is not possible, substitute family care should be attempted prior to children being taken to orphanages or transit camps. Safety, affection and stability are some of the key characteristics of a good short-term placement in a substitute family.

CHECKLIST: documentation of children

1. Devise a training programme with emphasis on listening skills, gaining the trust of children, addressing their fears and communicating with them. Draw up guidelines on interviewing and discussing options with children.

2. Concurrently devise forms for recording the information. Test these out by using them with a number of children, staff and community leaders and make sure the questions are clear and culturally appropriate.

3. Prepare the communities and the children. Expect resistance to documentation and address it through public meetings, with community leaders or heads of institutions, followed by smaller meetings with children. Allow plenty of opportunity for questions. Promise and ensure confidentiality.

4. Draw up a system for monitoring documentation. Observe a small number of documentations and examine some completed forms. Feedback constructively on areas that need improving.

5. Design a system for the printing, stockpiling and distribution of forms, for the processing of information collected in the relevant locations and for an administrative system which has efficiency and accountability built into it.

6. Decide on the appropriateness of using photographs and computers, having weighed up advantages and disadvantages.

BAD PRACTICE IN DOCUMENTATION

Example A: Too quick and insensitive.

The tracing worker arrived in a landrover and attracted a lot of attention. The displaced people thought he had come to bring them aid. He bustled around, called a quick meeting, and documented fifteen children in less than a hour by firing questions at them in front of everyone. He then left.

Example B: Children are the objects and not the subjects of the documentation. They were neither involved nor consulted.

This tracing worker explained what he was doing to the community. Slowly they brought out the separated children who stood in front of him, hanging their heads. The tracing worker then addressed all his questions to the eldest males. All the documentation was done without the children being asked a single question.

Example C: Children often cannot exercise choice in public.

The female tracing worker followed the guidelines on choice which said she had to ask the child where she wanted to live. But she did it in front of the substitute family the child was living with plus another twenty or so people who had gathered round to listen to the discussion. The child did not reply.

TRACING

TRACING STAFF DESCRIBE THEIR WORK

Three accounts which show how difficult tracing work can be:

1. "The three children were orphans and we were looking for the uncle. After four days of travelling and asking and travelling and asking we found him in town. He led us to his home. He had just returned from far away where he had fled to. He was just building a mud hut with grass thatch. It had one room. The man had no bedding. He was a widower and all his four children were dead. The local school was not yet functioning. The uncle said he could not afford to have the three children. We advised him to work hard and build a strong home and grow more food. We would keep the children for some more time, and then we would return them to him."

2. "We traced his grandmother, after walking up so many hills. She informed us that the mother was still alive, although living far away, remarried to another man. The father too was alive, but was ill with Aids. The grandmother had only one small room and no land. The child was returned to the Home while we thought about what to do."

3. "He said his father was well known. And indeed when we got there, the first group of men we asked did in fact know him. Unfortunately he was dead. However, they directed us to where the elder sons were staying. The brother of 21 said he could not manage to look after him. Also, since he had been staying in a city, he would find the village very difficult. But the young child did not want to go back to the institution. He pleaded. We supported his argument with the older brother. We gave him advice like a parent would. We emphasised the child belonged to him, and to no one else. He should mould him into a good citizen. The child was also encouraged to be a good boy, ready to listen to advice and be respectful and ready to work on the farm with an iron hand. We left him there."

Tracing staff need to assess what is in the child's best interests. In none of these three examples did the extended family feel able to take the children. The assessment by the tracing staff concluded in the first example that the children's best interests would be with the uncle, but time was needed to enable him to recreate a family environment. In the second example, the parents would be contacted by the tracing staff to assess which of the three relatives who had been found, would provide the best for the child. In the third example the boy himself made his own assessment and the staff supported him.

Tracing in this chapter refers specifically to the search for the family of a separated child. This starts when the documentation is done and finishes either when a family is located which is able to keep the child, or when the decision is made to give up searching and an alternative long-term placement is needed. It can take months or even years. The International Committee of the Red Cross estimates, worldwide, a 20 per cent success rate for adult tracing – and less for children. In some situations success rates can be much higher. And where wars or disasters are very local, tracing success can be very high. The Ethiopian tracing team traced some 90 per cent of children's families after the drought in Wollo.

TYPES OF TRACING

There are various types of tracing, which may be divided in a number of ways:

- **tracing in war conditions, and tracing after a war is ended.** The latter makes travel easier and more methods of tracing possible; or
- **urban tracing and rural tracing.** Different methods are useful in urban tracing from rural tracing; or
- **tracing within a province, across provinces, and across national borders.** This is a division that may be useful when different staff are involved at these three levels and information needs to be passed efficiently from one set of personnel to another; or
- **children's wish to trace, and children's wish not to trace.** In most emergency situations children are desperate to be with their families, but it can be left too late. If the tracing is done five years after children have settled in with substitute families or several years after they have been placed in relatively affluent children's homes with access to secondary education, there may be resistance. And with resistance, tracing is much more difficult and requires different methods again.

Different types of tracing will be taking place simultaneously in many countries, and methods need to be adapted accordingly.

The probability of failure in tracing the child's family needs to be estimated and taken into consideration when deciding on tracing methods. The other important reason for caution is that 'success' – the return of a child to family members who are not parents or grandparents with a secure standard of living or an uncle or aunt with culturally clearly demarcated responsibility for the child plus a reasonable standard of living – is often problematic.

GOOD PRACTICE IN TRACING

Good practice requires tracing to:
- trace families without the children taking part in the tracing;
- verify the details;
- assess whether the family are willing and able to take the child;
- plan the reunification;
- prepare the family;
- prepare the child, re-assess needs and wishes; and
- decide whether to reunify the child.

In actual practice, however, much tracing tends to consist of the following:
- children accompanying tracers;
- children being reunified with any member of the family without an assessment of the situation;
- children not given time to prepare or the opportunity to plan their future jointly.

There is often a large gap between good practice and the reality of much tracing. Bad tracing practice may include the following features:

Children

- Not understanding children's behaviour – their worries, their lies, their resistance.

System

- Waiting. Not taking any initiative.
- Bad planning and no planning for individual children.
- Inappropriate recording – no record of day-to-day activities.

Management

- Poor management – of team and resources and forms etc.
- Ineffective training and supervision.

Politics

- Not using community leaders, not understanding cultural practices.
- Politicisation – tribalism – seeing children as belonging to the enemy.

SOME COMMON WAYS OF TRACING

The main constraints on tracing are the security situation of a country, the ease of travel and the budgets available. The resulting methods are grouped broadly into tracing which is based on extensive travel, and tracing which involves sending information rather than people to distant places.

Tracing through travel

It may be part of social or community workers' jobs to trace families in their areas. This may mean that they receive a copy of the documentation form and they set off – probably on local buses, but possibly on motorbikes donated through an aid programme – to try and locate the family. Alternatively the specialist tracing team might be responsible for this.

The first step may be to try and locate the area, then narrow it down to the market that is closest to the village where the child might come from. The tracing staff may then stop at the market and ask people if they know the family named or, if they have a photograph, whether anyone recognises the child. Sometimes a member of the family is at the market, selling or buying some goods. Other times they are known, but are not present. Or they are known to be dead. Frequently however there is no news, and the tracing must continue – or retrace its steps and start again, looking for different clues as to where the family may have lived or be living.

Travelling tracing involves putting together bits of incomplete information to try and make a complete picture. Various skills are needed:

- the willingness to travel widely, sometimes in dangerous areas, often in poor weather conditions, often with slow and unreliable transport, and being met with suspicion and resistance by local people;
- knowledge of local areas, so that even small bits of information – "it's a cross roads with seven trees" or "there is a mosque and it is near the river" or "up on the hill past the army barracks" – lead to the identification of an area;
- lateral thinking – guesses, deduction, hypotheses, hunches, analyses of where people flee to and who is left behind: "it was in the early part of the war and people then still fled towards the sea", "they are a nomadic family and we must find out where they are likely to be in this season", or "that transit camp in the capital is likely to have people who fled from the same area – let us ask there".

The problems of tracing through travel

The main problems of tracing through travel:

- staff may be resistant to leave their offices and travel;
- the further away the village to be located is, the more likely the staff are to delay a visit. There is usually no incentive built in to compensate for the bad travel conditions, time away or possible safety risks;
- staff give up too early when they are told someone is dead. If someone knows a parent is dead, the person may also know about other relatives, or neighbours who might know of other relatives, or the relevant community leader who might help tracing grandparents or uncles who have moved away. Every piece of information leads potentially to another one.

Office-based tracing

Office-based tracing methods may be useful where it is not possible for tracing staff to travel. Office-based tracing includes:

- **Advertising in newspapers.** This may be useful as a place to publish the photograph of a separated child. This is particularly effective if the child has been separated/lost very recently and if the photograph is a good one. Newspapers are least useful where the separation took place many years ago and a long way away. In some countries papers will publish pictures and short stories for free – perhaps they see it as a combination of social service plus free cover. In other countries papers charge commercial advertising rates – making the whole exercise expensive and not usually value-for-money. Attempts should be made to negotiate a better arrangement.
- **Advertising on radio.** This has variable success depending on many factors: the cost of batteries in the rural areas, whether names are known when the separation took place and so on. Radios rely on accuracy. A message may be successful if there is enough local detail and specific information to help identify the family – even if, as in the example which follows, the family name is a very common one. Example: 'Mr Moyo is wanted, whose seven-year-old son was found nine miles outside the capital on the main road leading south, who was separated on Sunday 7 September after church when the bombing began near St Mary's Church.'

  Much less helpful messages are those which reel off a list of names in quick succession, with little or no details. They may also stigmatise parents and children. And sometimes in wars, owning a radio is a death warrant: people are often killed for radios or watches.

If there are large numbers of children who need families tracing, it is better to assume that the families are themselves searching for the children and to broadcast how they should search: ie register with the District Commissioner, local school, health clinic or whoever is coordinating the tracing. The radio message should be short and simple, and should be repeated frequently. A system should then be developed for registering the children sought. Registration should be thorough – detailed verification of the relationship and the circumstances of the separation are needed. These need to be matched against what the child has said. Children should never – never – be handed over to adults without ascertaining that the child and adult are related. A system of verification is needed, to protect children from adults who are looking for cheap farm labour, for teenagers to fight men's wars, for house-girls to look after children or for second wives. This is why no radio message or tracing system should imply that adults can simply present themselves at a transit camp or orphanage and return home with unknown and unrelated children.

- **Advertising on television.** This is a specialised form of advertising, potentially very expensive and restricted to the urban middle classes. But where agreements can be made for 'free tracing' to be done on special programmes, then it may be a useful method, even if it has variable or low response – because families who have lost children often do not have access to televisions. A risk to be considered is that showing children, particularly where they are girls, is open to abuse of adults posing as relatives in order to get house-girls or second wives. Very strict systems of verification have to be built into any use of television – taking local conditions including the bribability of individuals into account.

- **Advertising through posters.** Where a tracing system relies on photographs rather than visits, posters of several children – 12 or even 24 smiling faces looking out of a poster can be displayed in public places. Temples, churches, clinics, schools, market places, administrative offices are all good places. A permanent exhibition of photographs at the district or provincial office of the Ministry of Welfare might be useful, if it is combined with publicity to inform people that they should go there if they are looking for a child from their village, and they should be told there will be a system of verification. It should be clear the children are not being offered to anyone who has a home and wants one.

- **Meetings.** These are always useful because they can inform, educate, sensitise. But meetings have to follow accepted community practices and be called by people known in the community and have to be introduced and supported by local leaders. Tracing has negative connotations in many countries where children are abducted, kidnapped and used by all sides of a war; meetings have to convince people that tracers are in effect attempting the opposite – the reunification and recreation of family bonds.

Traditional chiefs and leaders are important people to involve in tracing – they often have memories which are deeper than wells and which can draw lineages to identify family members over several generations. They also have power and authority over people – power to call meetings, and authority to support tracing programmes. Working without them is not just inefficient, but also dangerous. If they were to advise the community to resist tracing attempts, this would be hard to undo.

TAKING CHILDREN ON TRACING TRIPS

It is often tempting to take children on pro-active tracing trips because if they are successful, then they may save a return trip. It makes reunification cheaper, and indeed, tracing with children is often justified by reference to the difficulties of tracing on a very limited budget. Tracing may also seem easier if the child is taken with the tracing team. They may recognise parts of the environment which they were not able to describe – a tree on the way to school, the spot where they used to get off the bus, a river where they used to play. They may identify the right way to the village or house; they may be an active partner in the tracing expedition.

So why is it generally not good practice to include them from the beginning? The main reasons for not taking children along on tracing trips generally are:

- tracing itself is very emotionally demanding, unsettling and frightening;
- for those who cannot find their families it is exposure to another form of violence, one they experience en route;
- for those who can find relatives, time to prepare on both sides helps lay better foundations for a long-term relationship.

The practical advantages of finding villages or homes have to be weighed against the emotional cost of another rejection, a failure, the end to the child's hopes and dreams. Children may sit in hot and dusty landrovers for days, highly emotional about the anticipated reunion, desperately hoping their family is still there, alive and welcoming. In practice, for many the homes are never found, the family is dead, or where there are remaining relatives they may be too poor to feed themselves or too distraught to want the responsibility of another child. For the child this is a difficult experience, another rejection, a brutal blow to the hopes that have probably helped him through the separation. While the older children can be prepared – a little – for this outcome, and helped through it when it does occur, for the younger ones it is an experience that adds to the emotional devastation already experienced.

Reunification may be straightforward: relatives may be delighted to see the child, they may have surplus food, they may not see any difficulty in taking the child and bringing them up as their own. In practice, however, for many the response is a mixture of pleasure, surprise and gratitude that the child has been spared – combined with the feeling they cannot possibly feed another mouth, they have nothing material to offer the child, the child would be better off in an orphanage or elsewhere under government care and they would prefer not to have the child.

A negotiation follows, where the tracer and the family question each other's positions through a series of speeches, rhetorical questions and both sides frequently call on the ancestors to help. To the child, it feels like neither side wants him. If it was difficult being separated, it is as difficult or more difficult being reunited yet feeling unwanted. There is no hope left. If children can be spared this negotiation and if children and families can be prepared for the realities of a family reunification then reunification has a better chance of success.

Where parents themselves are found, they too need time to prepare and to think through the changes that have happened since separation. Both child and parent need to understand that the child is no longer the same as before. It is probably an emotionally battered, violated and frightened child that is being returned, and will need much time, effort and love to settle.

INTERNATIONAL TRACING

In many countries, wars or disasters mean people flee into neighbouring countries and tracing can mean seeking children or parents who have fled across national borders. The International Committee of the Red Cross (ICRC) can be contacted, or the national Ministries of Social Welfare in the other countries – or embassies or international agencies working with refugees. In all cases, all the information gained from thorough documentation needs to be forwarded, with requests for advertising in refugee settlements or in national newspapers and/or with pro-active tracing requests.

Generally if there is an IDTR programme or system in the neighbouring countries, then the question becomes one of synchronising the forms, the information sought and the format of the records. This is a major task since it is likely that different organisations will be involved in each country and possibly several organisations in each, all possibly using different forms, and all reluctant to change 'their' forms or approaches. But creating one workable system out of a plethora of experiences is the key to international tracing. A good understanding of legal issues and transnational refugee policy is also vital, if programmes involve sending people back across borders.

ADMINISTRATION OF TRACING

Good practice in the administration of tracing requires the following:

- **An effective system of document collection, storage and analysis is essential.** Documentation and the analysis of the documentation for use in tracing is tedious. A mass of detail is gathered, and this is time-consuming, and requires patience and obsessive care.
- **Selection of staff with the skills and willingness to administer such a system is likewise essential.**
- **Practical judgments must be made on how to file and how to retrieve information.** Should it be alphabetically by the child's name? Or the family's name? Or should it be done by province or even village of origin? Or in date order? The most useful kind of filing can only be decided once decisions on tracing methods have been made.
- **A back-up system has to be decided on.** Most tracing starts in war or disaster conditions, with instability, uncertainty and upheaval surrounding the plans for tracing. The offices from which tracing takes place may be overrun, files may be destroyed, computers and discs may be stolen, and tracing staff may be blown up by unexploded landmines. A 'back-up' system of records, probably a duplicate set at another office – district, provincial or capital – is therefore essential. Otherwise it is all too easy for months and months of documentation to be lost in one incident.
- **Long-term planning is required.** Some families may be traced very quickly, but most will not. The system being set up should stay effective, growing in size and complexity, for several years. Information is likely to come in from more and more places, needing categorisation and cross-referencing. A well developed tracing programme will be able to integrate routinely newly found children documented in and by local villages, documentations in neighbouring refugee and transit camps, and even children within the ICRC system.

- **The system must be designed to allow for cross-referencing** from the two main sources of information: children talking about their families, and families talking about their children. Whether or not the tools of modern technology are used – Polaroid cameras, posters with photographs, computer matching, chartering aeroplanes – the essence of a good tracing system should be to provide easily accessible, detailed information, which can be cross-referenced for tracing.
- **Long-term storage should be ensured.** After several years, when the international donors have withdrawn, and formal tracing has nearly ceased, the door should still stay open. The information needs to be kept somewhere, so that if and when families come looking for children who have been documented five or ten years ago, the information should still be accessible, retrievable, useful.

CHECKLIST: practical points and hints

- Changes in addresses.
- Stability/security of areas.
- Inaccessibility of areas.
- Age: with young children seek out who came with them.
- How to get information from the deaf and dumb? And what to do with children with disabilities where their families did not want them?
- Unwillingness of some parents to keep children: financial problems; or children's behaviour was difficult; or remarriage.
- Commitment of tracers may be very variable.
- Problems of transportation.

CHECKLIST: practical management problems

- People don't go to work. They are not paid enough, and sometimes not paid at all.

- Cars are stolen. Petrol is rationed, unavailable.

- 'Social worker' just means anyone who works with children.

- The tracing team and the orphanage staff refuse to talk to each other.

- Tracing staff may not be enthusiastic about follow-up work because of the travel involved.

- Tracing itself does not work in most provinces, let alone follow-up.

- Files sit there for months. No one does anything. There is no management that asks for results.

VERIFICATION

Tracing needs always to go hand in hand with verification. The system for verification is quite straightforward: forms and methods should be used which mirror the information collected during the documentation. Someone claiming to be an 'uncle' of a child should be asked the same questions as the child was: the names of all the various members of the family, where they lived before, the nature of the separating incident and so on. This should be matched against the information from the child.

The aim of verification is to make sure that the child is returned to the appropriate family. This is a form of protection for the child, which needs to be built into the tracing system, so that people cannot access, remove, or buy children who are without families in the midst of an emergency. Most of the time its real value is as a deterrent. When people come to know that they have to fill in forms, sign them, and if there is doubt about them, then to go and get letters of confirmation from community leaders, this acts as a very strong deterrent against attempts to gain children by false means. But sometimes systems of verification act as more than deterrents – they are the means by which people who are looking for boy soldiers, cheap labour on farms, free house-girls, additional 'wives' or other forms of abuse, can be identified.

In countries which use the more reactive method – ie distributing lists or posters, rather than seeking out families – one of the main aims of detailed documentation is for use in verification. The detailed documentation cannot be circulated publicly – it is most useful when someone has been traced or someone has come forward. In countries where much of the tracing involves seeking out members of the family, the detailed information is important in planning where to search for each member – and each will be tried until someone is found.

Where children have not been able to give much information, perhaps because they are young or traumatised, the verification process can be used in reverse. Photographs of the relatives can be taken, together with their children. The child can then later be asked if they recognise them – and younger children will often be more likely to recognise the children rather than the adults. The relatives can also be asked to describe situations or circumstances which the child might remember – and these are described by the tracers to the child. Sometimes the child's whole face lights up with the pleasure of the memory, from her past. At other times, many memories to do with the past have been suppressed or erased. Hoping has been too painful, and it was easier to blank it all out. Verification thus has to be done carefully, and lack of recognition and lack of verification noted. Both need further investigation – relatives can be asked for supporting evidence, while the child often just needs time in order to re-connect with the memories that have been swept aside. Messages and visits help.

ASSESSMENT

Having traced and verified the family, an assessment of the family and community situation is needed. This assessment has social and economic dimensions, and also involves choice by the child.

The social dimension of assessment

The social dimension involves the person carrying out the tracing answering the following question: Does the family show some positive feelings to the child? Does the family show some interest in having the child? Are there problems within the family which might need discussing (such as alcoholism, a stepparent unwilling to have the child, outright hostility towards the child – either because of something the child did, or because he is the son of someone who for example was on the 'other side' during the war). If there are problems, can they be solved with the involvement of local community leaders?

The economic dimension of assessment

The majority of families who will be receiving these children will be poor. Very poor. Many will have lost all their assets – animals, machinery, houses – and will be struggling to start from next to nothing to grow food for the next season. But some will be even poorer than the poverty of the 'norm' – they may be totally destitute, and not even beginning the long process of re-establishing food production.

The economic conditions one is planning to return the child to need to be assessed very carefully. There are situations where placing children into destitution has more negative effects than leaving them in their previous situations. Families often seek to 'shed' children when they are destitute. They may be placed with more affluent families, related or not. They may be sent to towns to get work. They may be married off or have turned to prostitution. A strict hierarchy of access to food may be established, and more distantly related children, or children who have been away under the protection of others, will be fed last, if at all. Either some intervention is desirable in the economic situation – or placement needs to be deferred or re-thought.

Choice

And lastly there is the question of the child's right to choice – what rights do these children have to choose whether they are reunified and to whom? This important area will be discussed in the next section.

CHECKLIST: tracing procedures

- Plot the location of the origin of the children on a map, once children have been documented. Draw up from this a tracing plan, with the allocation of resources to different kinds of tracing in different parts of the country.

- Draw up a list of tracing methods and choose the most appropriate ones for each situation. Tracing in war conditions, in peace time, in rural and urban areas all need different methods.

- Decide on the balance between office-based tracing and tracing involving extensive travel. Extensive travel is often very effective, but time-consuming, expensive and not possible when wars are ongoing.

- Facilitate informal networks which enable families to trace their lost children. Publicise methods for families to use in their own tracing.

- Agree a policy about whether and when children should accompany tracing staff. Take into account that it is unsettling and frightening. Prepare children – for the emotional difficulties en route as well as the uncertain conclusions.

- Tracing staff should prepare children after a successful tracing has been achieved. Children should understand they may be going to a displaced and incomplete family, very poor and with all members under stress. Families too need to be prepared, to understand that the child also has changed, and will need patience and love while she learns to settle.

- Tracing systems must have long-term plans for record keeping, plans which will survive both attacks on offices as well as withdrawal of funds as donor organisations move elsewhere. Back-up systems are important.

- A system of verification needs to be designed. It is a form of protection for separated children, to ensure they are reunited with the right family. It should act both as a deterrent and as a means of identifying those who seek to acquire children by false means.

- The last step in tracing requires an assessment of the family to be made. The social dimension of the assessment involves assessing whether there are problems within the family which need addressing. The economic dimension assesses whether there is economic destitution which would harm the child. The line between poverty and destitution is often hard to identify; but the aim of the assessment remains to assess the safety and wisdom of placing a child with the family in their particular circumstances.

PLACEMENT

THE IMPORTANCE OF BELONGING

Hassan had escaped to a neighbouring country where he had lived for many years. When the war was over, he was returned, as a young man of seventeen. When I tried to interview the boy in my office he could hardly speak his own language any more and he was not willing to talk much. He knew his parents were dead. We decided to try and find his maternal uncle. We drove for a long time and he was very quiet. But when we neared the village where his uncle might be, he declared "I think I am on my way home." When we reached the market place just before the village, the boy suddenly got very excited and declared "I am a member here now". The vehicle stopped and he jumped out and started introducing himself to a large crowd of people who were gathered under a mango tree. He suddenly spoke fluently. His uncle immediately recognised him and called him by name. They were both overjoyed. All the people had thought the boy was dead and there was a very big celebration and they all thanked the ancestors for saving him.

(Tracer's report from Uganda)

INTRODUCTION

In an emergency situation, where separation is a recent event, the main aim of a tracing programme is finding the original family and reunifying the child. In other situations, where the separation took place some time ago, the aim may have changed. As time passes the probability of successful tracing decreases, and with this comes a broadening of objectives. While the first goal is to find the family of origin, the aim is to find a long-term placement for the child, a place where she can spend what is left of her childhood growing up in safety and stability.

In this section we first look at what is called 'family reunification', ie the return of the child to the family. We then turn to how safeguards can be built into the successful placement of children. The third section looks at some of the advantages and disadvantages of providing kits as part of a reunification programme. The fourth section focuses on the need for after-care. The fifth looks at situations where reunification cannot or should not take place, while the last examines placements of children with other families, called 'substitute' families or foster families, when related families cannot be traced.

FAMILY REUNIFICATION

Reunifying a child with her family can mean many things: the direct return to the same family members; return to live with all new relations; return to new places.

Direct return to the same family

The simplest form of reunification is the direct return of a child to the members of the family she was living with before the separation. In the simplest reunification she is also returned to the same place they were living in before – displacement of the family was temporary and they are all back together.

In this example the people are the same and the place is the same. But nevertheless the first impression of 'sameness' is illusory: the child has had some very frightening experiences. She has been without protection for a period of time. She may have been beaten, abused, raped. She is in many ways not the same child she was before. And the family has changed too. Each member has had to develop survival strategies for themselves and for their relatives, sometimes with uncomfortable consequences. They may have had to choose which of their children should live and which should die. The mother may have had to turn to prostitution to survive. The father may have had to betray his community, his tribe, his religion, his caste in order to stay alive.

Reunification is not, therefore, a return to the situation that was before, but rebuilding, recreating a family, with new experiences which the family needs to come to terms with. It means assessing whether the reunification should take place and if it should, trying to build safeguards into a reunification, to help it become a successful one.

Returning to different people in different places

In other kinds of family reunification, the new home is even more different. The child is not reunified with the family members she was living with before. She may be reunified with other family members, in other places. She may hardly know them. They may have conflicting feelings about family obligations and struggles to support themselves. Social and economic pressures may be pushing in different directions, with the child caught in the middle. The living situation is also essentially new, although the kinship it is based on is not. This kind of reunification also requires some kind of assessment as to its safety and desirability and then safeguards to be built in, to help the placement to be a successful one.

CHILDREN'S VIEWS ON WHY THEY WERE GOING TO BE REUNIFIED

Anna: I want to see my mother again.

Joseph: The government no longer wants us.

Cheepo: The soldiers have eaten many people but not my grandmother and I am going to her.

Rahim: These people are trying to help us.

Fred: I want to see my village again, where I played with my friends.

Elisabeth: There is no more food here for us.

Kamal: I do not understand.

Jemal: They have not told us.

Patience: They found my uncle and he wants me.

Zina: They will chase us away if we do not go.

Mohamed: Because the government said so.

Molla: The rains have come so we can grow food again.

Julius: That is where my land is.

Nyerengo: They say the land has stopped bleeding and it is safe.

Comment: It is very important to explain to the children as much as possible: what is going to happen, why it is going to happen, when it is going to happen. Often it is necessary to explain the same thing several times and then to check that they have understood it.

SAFEGUARDS

It is useful to identify two kinds of vulnerability early on. First is the vulnerable child, who might be particularly emotional or sensitive, who might have a history of difficulties; or who might have an attachment with an adult that will be very painful to break. Second is the vulnerable situation, where the child is being returned to very distant relatives or to a village in the midst of the war or some other kind of environmental vulnerability. These two conditions may need extra time and preparation to make the reunification a successful one.

It is in this context that many tracing programmes have attempted to build various small safeguards into the reunification. These consist of:

- making the arrival of the child into a publicly witnessed event;
- expecting the receiving family to confirm in writing, in public, their willingness to look after the child;
- entrusting a community leader to monitor the settling in of the child and advise on any problems arising;
- and sometimes building follow-up visits and interviews by tracing workers into the programme.

A public event

The return of the child to her home (either to their old home or to a new one) should be made into a public event. Community leaders should be called to witness the return, neighbours too should be encouraged to come and welcome the child. Wider family who live close by can also be invited. It should be an important event for the family, acknowledging a new household member and establishing publicly the rights of the child to receive care and protection in his new home. Some cultures mark important events with music and dancing and singing. Others use prayers, or make offerings to ancestors or Gods. Whatever is culturally appropriate is good. It marks a big event, an important occasion. Only exceptionally is it more prudent not to mark the event – for example if it puts the child in danger from previous abductors.

The tracing worker should spend time on the reunification, both taking part in the celebrations and talking to the adults about the child, where she has been living, what her needs might be. The family should talk about what they can offer the child – ie schooling, what they expect the child to do (work in the fields?), and a picture of the future should be jointly presented. The child should be encouraged to participate, ask questions, raise worries – although in practice many are overwhelmed and say little or nothing. Tracing staff need to act as intermediaries here – giving the children confidence to talk, interpreting the situation to them, helping them to settle. The reunification is the new start, and needs to be acknowledged as this.

Confirmation in writing

Families should be expected to confirm in writing their willingness to take the child and have her living with them. The less close the family tie, the more important this confirmation is. It is least necessary for natural parents and most useful when the child is placed with distant relatives. Most reunification programmes use a form which has an 'I promise...' section. This is read out to the family, in front of all the visitors and community leaders, and the head of the family signs the promise, using his or her thumbprint if necessary. In many communities signing an undertaking is a big event, sometimes even a threatening event. It usually has the effect of creating a moral bond, a social bond, a publicly acknowledged economic bond with economic obligations.

Entrusting a community leader to monitor

The importance of having community leaders present at the reunification cannot be over-stressed. Their role may differ in the detail: in some programmes they are asked to sign the reunification form as having been witnessed by a person in authority, in others their role is less clearly defined – they sign nothing, but see everything. What is however essential is that they have a clearly defined role for the future. The tracing staff need to evoke this role, to turn to the family and ask them, publicly, to share any problems they have in the future about the child, with the community leaders. The tracing staff need to convey this to the child too. If problems arise which cannot be sorted out within the family, then the child must have someone to turn to. And the community leaders should be asked to take the initiative and see the child while she is settling in, to help her adjust to the new situation and to help the family adjust to her. The child, in turn can also be asked to choose someone, from those present, who will be a person she can turn to, someone to talk about problems to.

In most cases, community leaders monitor without needing to intervene. Their role is one of guidance, of advice, of making both sides feel they are not alone with any problem which may arise. But sometimes the community leader does have a more important role. The child may run away, and when found, may allege being mistreated or beaten or discriminated against or abused. It falls to the community leaders to listen to both sides and to make a decision. The child may need to return with some monitoring of the situation or she may need to be moved to other members of the family or even an unrelated 'foster' family. Inheritance disputes also often need local community leaders' help to be resolved. A returning child does displace some other member of the family's access to inherited land.

Visits by tracing staff

Some programmes have built in visits for tracing workers to undertake after reunification. Clearly where social workers have travelled two thousand miles across a country to place a child, they are not likely to be able to return in a month to check on her well-being. It would be an expensive use of scarce resources. But where it is district tracing workers who place children in families living in their districts, it is more feasible to build in such visits.

KITS

In many, but not all family tracing programmes, a kit usually containing one or more of the following: basic foodstuffs, clothes, school material, tools and seeds, is offered the family. The items will vary according to the needs of the people living in the areas. The aim of this kit is to help the family through the transition period of absorbing an additional member to be fed, clothed and educated.

But the kit has another important aim, at least as important as short-term material help. It is a symbolic gift, that goes with the child, that is associated with the child, that helps the child be accepted. Symbols, rituals, gifts, all these play very important roles in societies all over the world, and the bringing of a gift to the receiving family is an acknowledgement of the care they are going to offer, the love they are going to extend, and the sacrifices they are going to make for the child. A kit is not, of course, a substitute for a family needs assessment or for after-care.

Problems with kits

There are nevertheless problems with kits:
- **Financial issues.** Is it worth spending money on kits when it could be spent on another reunification? This depends on the size of the tracing budget in relation to the size of the tracing need. And it is part of the 'quantity' versus 'quality' debate. Should one maximise numbers even if

ten or twenty per cent of reunifications lead to serious problems? Kits are part of 'quality' tracing – it is doing just a bit more than the minimum, but less than offering individually assessed after-care.

- **Questions of targeting.** Should families which are relatively well off still be given kits? This again is partly a financial decision. If, as in many war situations, most receiving families are near destitution, it seems a waste of time and resources to try to identify the handful of families who are a little better off. If however there are sizeable numbers of families that are prosperous, then some kind of targeting of kits to the non-prosperous ones may be sensible. The costs of operating a means-tested system need also to be weighed up. It means training staff to carry out needs assessment, to account for decisions to give or withhold kits, and it also means designing procedures for appeal by families and for investigation when families protest their need. If assessments are made, they should be made at the tracing stage.

- **Should the kit be child-centred or family-centred?** Should it include a plate, a mug, a saucepan; or maybe include a goat, to raise the nutrition of the whole family; or agricultural implements? In many places children have few or no personal belongings, so giving them too much singles them out as different and privileged. However, having one or two per-sonal items does mean, again symbolically, that the children who may have lost so much of their family, their parents and siblings, do have something, however small, that is theirs. A mixed kit of items is often the best solution.

- **Is it a temptation for the tracing staff or orphanage staff to keep the kits or sell them,** rather than give them to the children? Sometimes it clearly is, especially when as in some situations government employees are paid so little and so unreliably. The solution is to make it difficult for anyone to divert the kit items along the way: the tracing system should have procedures for accounting for the goods right up to the point where the family receives them and the community leaders sign the form accepting the child plus the itemised kit.

- **Is the whole idea of a kit a materialistic, western creation?** Shouldn't it be enough to bring the child? Is it a bribe, a false incentive, a harmful addition? All these arguments have been made at various times, and as always there is a grain of truth in all of them. But there are arguments which seem to outweigh these. It is a useful materialistic addition. In areas with water shortages, people clap when they are given a jerrycan. Families appreciate it, remember it, use it. Children too are proud of what 'they' brought to the family. They feel just a little less of a burden. And when the placement breaks down, children often sell what is left of the goods, and use the money to run away. So the kit also functions as a resource to fall back on. Families also use it that way – they may sell the items in order to buy food, when they have no money left.

EXAMPLES OF KITS

Example A:

- hoe
- bedsheet
- jerrycan
- basin
- slasher
- saucepan
- mattress
- mug
- panga
- plate
- blanket

Example B:

- beans
- rice
- groundnuts
- or tinned milk for babies (without their mothers) 2 years.

Example C:

- a goat

Example D:

- fertiliser and seeds

Examples of what to take with children:

- Personal belongings.
- Medical records.
- School records.
- Letters for administrative authorities if necessary.
- Any documentation relating to other family members traced.
- Any documents about the child's recent experiences that would be useful to them.

Examples of problems with kits:

- That boy is seen as a rich boy with his kit. The other children do not talk to him. They steal his things.
- It identifies him as the rich city boy coming home with his bad habits.
- In the eyes of some of the neighbours it seems to reward families for abandoning their children.

AFTER-CARE

> **"It's not sending home but making a home"**

Tracing is often seen as an emergency programme, and this makes questions about after-care difficult to raise. The assumption is sometimes made that once a family is successfully traced and the child placed, that is the end of the problem, and the end of the programme. But successful tracing means the beginning of a new problem. It's now a question of how to 'make' the child and family and the community fit. Younger children often fit in more easily than older ones: they adapt more easily to new routines and new environments. Older children may be more set in the ways of the camp or institution.

It is important for people working on a tracing programme not to see finding a family for a child as the ultimate goal. It makes it difficult to question, once a member of a family has been found, whether the child should be placed with them or not; and, if placed, what after-care needs the family may have. Reunification reports, follow-up reports and evaluations all suggest that there are many more needs to address. After-care means asking at the time of placement the question: What help does the child need to 'make a home' without creating a long-term dependency?

AFTER-CARE DILEMMAS

- A ten-year-old was reunified with his mother who was lame. The school is 18 kms away and the homestead has no food.
- A 12-year-old was reunified with an uncle who then threatened to kill him for eating too much of the beans given as his kit. The placement was considered unsafe.
- A follow-up report said: "This child looks sickly and traumatised. The family is overburdened and the aunts are very old."
- A follow-up report said: "This child needs a lot of attention which may not be possible due to too many young dependants in the family. He is upsetting the whole family."
- A follow-up report said: "This eight-year-old is reunified with her mentally handicapped mother. They cannot cope on their own."

FAMILY NEEDS ASSESSMENT

A family needing assessment will enable tracing staff to decide whether and what kinds of after-care is needed.

Some of the questions a family needs assessment can ask, may include the following:

- Does the family have enough food?
- Are the living conditions satisfactory?
- Is the village safe?
- Does the child have a clear role in the family?
- Is the child fully accepted?
- Does the child have access to school?
- Is there health provision?
- Are there inheritance issues to address?

Economic issues

Some issues are economic. The problem may be school fees or uniform, copybooks, time lost on farming or the need for them to care for younger children. Children in some situations may not expect to go to school, but often children have been at school in refugee camps or in orphanages, and not going to school is a major problem. It can be important enough for some children to prefer to go back to the institutional setting rather than cease their education. Tracing programmes face a dilemma here: do they judge living in a family to be more important than the opportunities children would have from continuing education and can they say it is better for them this way? Or are they under some obligation to carry out a cost-benefit analysis and decide, since the children may well be worse off in the longer term, that the programme should try and arrange access to education? The latter may involve linking with other sponsors or funding the costs themselves.

There are many other issues to do with poverty and destitution. What if a family is so poor and so ill that having another family member pushes them over the destitution line? What if they have to starve some or all of the children? What if, on follow-up visits, the child is observed to have lost a lot of weight, and continues to do so? Does the programme insist on its boundaries as a tracing programme and not a development programme, and continue to count the growing malnutrition of the reunified child as a success?

Another common separation is when fathers take babies to a hospital or orphanage when the mother dies. These institutions may agree to take the babies for various periods, until they are older and more self-reliant.

Alternatively, institutions which offer 'after-care' or 'care in the community' increasingly are supplying dried milk and baby foods, until the baby is fully weaned and her food is cheaper for the family. These foods are invariably expensive in poor countries and economic reasons for separation can be addressed relatively easily. The supply of baby milk does not create dependency since the need is for a clearly limited period.

Social issues

The social needs of the family are also important. Few people escape some form of suffering during wars. But while beatings, capture, loss of family and property can all be talked about and shared, through the talking comes some healing, the suffering from being raped is often silent. Girls are frequently targets of rape, often performed in front of people and they have to live with the consequences. These may include medical consequences, infections, bleeding, internal damage. They always include emotional consequences, shame, guilt, anger, powerlessness. For girls it may mean sleeplessness or nightmares, overwhelming, fears and panics, feelings of badness and sadness.

All cultures see rape as a difficult subject to talk about and respond to. But there is a growing realisation that rape needs to be addressed, acknowledged and discussed. Sometimes this is addressed through the purification rights carried out to cleanse all evil. Sometimes it is done through community prayers to heal a child of all the violence in her past experience. Sometimes it is addressed in all women groups, or in discussions of health, or in one-to-one discussions between a 'substitute mother' figure and a child. It needs to be done in culturally appropriate ways, and ways that avoid further stigmatisation of the child. What seems important is that the child is helped to deal with her feelings, and she is met with understanding and non-judgmental responses. She needs to feel she can still be loved. Interim carers or long-term carers need to help her feel this.

What if the family consists of elderly grandparents who are unable to cope with an unruly teenage grandchild who has been badly traumatised by his experience of war? Does the programme again draw boundaries around tracing and reunification, whatever the experience after the reunification, or does it define its goal as successful reunification which means needing to address issues after the event? Does it problem-solve and try to explain the reasons for the child's behaviour to the grandparents and seek ways for the child to get involved and valued in the wider community, or does it say that is no longer part of its brief?

Both kinds of programmes exist. Narrow focused programmes which try to maximise the number of children reunified are often the programmes initially designed and funded. Broader programmes which consider longer-term success are the programmes which usually evolve from the recognition of all the problems which emerge. But there are also organisational differences among non-governmental organisations (NGOs) and situational differences in emergencies which lead to the emphasis either on quantity or quality. And since most organisations operate in the context of 'improving efficiency' it is increasingly difficult to move from reporting large numbers of successfully reunified children to reporting much smaller numbers for the same budgets. Perhaps quality issues and after-care needs to be built in from the beginning.

THE DECISION NOT TO REUNIFY

In every tracing programme there are some situations where the decision needs to be made that although family members can be traced, it is not ultimately in the child's best interests to live with them. This decision is not made lightly, indeed for both tracers and children it is often seen as a failure. There are broadly three kinds of situations: family unable, family unwilling or child unwilling. We look briefly at each.

If the family is unable to care for the child

The family may explain that they are unable to have a child because they have recently settled after many years of being displaced, they have no home, they sleep in the open, they have no crops, they live on next to nothing.

A variety of options exist in this situation.

- Sufficient 'kit' may be offered as an incentive to having the child, a kit that consists of long-term investment such as seeds.
- A delay in reunification may be agreed. For example if the family agrees to have the child back at the next harvest, then the programme will continue to look after the child at an orphanage till then.
- Other family members may be traced instead.

It would be sad if economic reasons were sufficient to keep a children from reunifying with their families. But material help must be balanced against the interests of other families in the area. It should not provide incentives for families to refuse their children.

Similar difficulties may arise if the family member traced is, for example, very disabled.

The family is unwilling to care for the child

A family may be unwilling to have a child perhaps because the child was involved in fighting or killing a member of the family; or possibly they think another relative is a closer relation and they should be given the child; or perhaps there was some problem in the past between the child's parents and these relatives, and this problem remains important. These kinds of 'historical' reasons, to do with events in the past which perhaps neither the tracer nor the child knows about, can interfere with reunification.

This is best approached by involving the community in a large discussion of the issues. Elders and traditional leaders may already know about the past events which are acting as obstacles and they may have the authority and wisdom with which to undo them. They can counsel forgiveness; they can advice on purification rites; they may call upon ancestors to mediate and guide. Traditional methods for addressing these kinds of obstacles are always best, but if these also fail, then the child will not be able to be reunified and it becomes very important to explain to him why it is not possible. The child may already feel rejected and abandoned and this is a repetition of an event on an already frail sense of identity. Counselling, explaining, trying to prevent the child feeling guilty and feeling unwanted and bad are very important. An alternative placement needs to be sought.

The child is unwilling to join the family

This situation is often difficult to interpret. The unwillingness of a child can include the 'normal' fear of a new situation, a change, a move. In most situations this fear should be expected. This guide has tried to stress the importance of educating, explaining and listening, and these three activities need to be applied here. Children should be asked why they are unwilling and each reason should be addressed seriously:

- Is it to do with leaving where they are now?
- Is it to do with what they might find when they get to the new place?

These two kinds of fears need to be separately identified and both talked about. It helps to give the child as much information about what they can expect as is possible. Often it is 'time' that helps too, giving children time to think over what a change would mean. Often observing friends and their peers being reunified helps them overcome their initial fears. Most children will show less fear as time goes on and they get used to the idea of a change.

For some children, however, their unwillingness can get worse and can include fears, for example, of past abuse re-occurring. These children often show different reactions from their friends and peers. They may get more withdrawn or they may become more disruptive. Both these kinds of behaviour need to be seen as signals for further talking and listening. Opportunities for children 'telling' should be created as early as possible. However even when these opportunities have been offered, children often leave it till the very last minute to explain, to disclose some deep fear they have. The seriousness of these fears has to be assessed, and in some cases the decision has to be made that it is not in the child's interest to return him to the situation.

Some programmes are reluctant to accept that children can choose not to be reunified. They may be surrounded by the effects of war, where everyone seems damaged and no one appears to have much of a choice about anything. It is in this context that many children appear to have been returned to their families and villages, crying with fear, resisting or withdrawn, feeling betrayed and helpless. This should not happen. Where there is widespread resistance to the reunification at the point at which it is happening, then the tracing programme has failed to educate, to explain, to work with children as partners. Children need to understand the world around them, and when they demonstrate through resistance that they do not understand or do not trust the decisions being made, then a programme has failed, or possibly not even tried to work with them.

IF CHILDREN REFUSE TO BE REUNIFIED

Step 1: Find out why
preference for urban life
guilt about siblings
anger about being abandoned
attachment to institution
family too poor
past abuse

Step 2: Address the issue
by counselling/explaining to child
by counselling/explaining to family and community

Step 3: Re-assess
is it in child's best interest?

Step 4: Arrange gradual reunification
weekend or week for child to assess
monitor

Step 5: Make alternative plans

PLACEMENT WITH A SUBSTITUTE FAMILY

Placing children in a substitute family may be a welcome relief to some children, who had been previously fending for themselves. But to some other children, particularly those who had been told that tracing of their families had failed or family members had been found but were unable to have them, substitute families may be met by fear, anger and resentment. These children are usually in the process of 'mourning' the family they have lost and need time and care. This should be explained to substitute families.

Placing children with substitute families is a difficult area to develop. There is little research which identifies when it works well and when it does not, and when it leads to exploitation of the children. One study in Mozambique found that of a hundred children studied in orphanages, in their own families and in substitute families, about twenty per cent, fairly evenly distributed between these three groups, were unhappy and wanted to move *. This is lower that expected – professionals' fears about substitute families leaving children open to neglect and abuse sometimes suggest even higher levels of concern. From Malawi for example, there are reports of large numbers of separated children running away or moving from family to family. But the reality is that no one really knows what makes a successful placement. Some programmes have used social workers as their initial foster families. Others have looked for willing families in the community. There are many factors to take into consideration.

Motivation

When families choose to look after a child, perhaps because they have found him while he was very young, and there is no financial incentive, the placement often works. Similarly, when families are given a child to care for, by the community elders who choose families who are responsible and reliable, then too the placement often works. However, financial incentives are problematic; they motivate people to take children for financial gain and the caring side is overshadowed by the wish for remuneration.

---

* Evaluation carried out by Josefa Langa, Alberto Mazamane and Helen Charnley, a team from the Secretariat of State for Social Action, Mozambique. 1991.

Standard of living

The standard of living of the family needs to be considered. Where families are poor, unrelated children may be the last to go to school, the first to go to work and the last to be fed. Where they are very poor, they may not be fed at all and even small children of three or four years might be expected to find their own food and/or earn money. Placements in very poor families are problematic; no matter how strong the motivation is, the caring often does not materialise.

Character

Some people are attracted to looking after separated children because these children are unprotected and easy to abuse. The most common form of abuse is economic, where children are made to labour on farms for excessively long hours at an early age. But there are other kinds of abuse, including being beaten and sexually abused. Much of this is, often, known in the community where the people live. A little questioning about the family seeking to care for a substitute child (of community leaders, neighbours, priests), prior to placement, would bring to light much of this information.

Screening

Each of these factors suggests clear guidance needs to be developed for the screening of placements with substitute families. The screening need not be very sophisticated. It needs:
- to ask questions about the family's motivation;
- assess whether the family can afford to feed and care for another child;
- ask community leaders for information about the character of the family.

Gradual placement

In many situations this is not possible, but where children can stay with sub-stitute families for a few days, return to orphanages and gradually get used to the family, placements are less frightening and more likely to be successful.

Planning the removal of children with care

Sometimes it will be necessary to remove children from particular family members, when they seem to be at risk. This should be considered carefully, discussed fully, and then alternative plans made. Other family members could be traced or a substitute family sought.

IDEAS FOR DEVELOPING AFTER-CARE

Workshops for adjustment

Arrange workshops for families who have had children returned. Discuss problems of adjustment. Look for community-based solutions and greater understanding of how the children are reacting.

Education programmes

A national policy on the education of reunited children is needed. For example:
- Free education will be offered for reunified children. Consider how this will be funded and how it can best be implemented.
- One-year scholarships will be offered to all reunified children. Consider how one year's free education will be funded and how best it can be implemented.
- There will be no overall provision, but individual cases will be forwarded for consideration to a NGO with a scholarship programme.

Health checks

In areas of drought or great poverty, health checks on children may be needed, such as weighing them monthly for the first three months or six months. A policy is needed about what to do with children who lose a lot of weight and/or get very ill.

Problem-solving mechanisms in the community

Policies may be needed on:
- what kinds of problems one should look out for; and
- what kind of solutions one is looking for.

The traditional or usual problem-solving mechanisms in the community may need to be identified and tracers trained to work with them to look for, understand and address them. Ultimately it is only the community leaders who need to address the problems. Most of the time tracing staff will visit too infrequently to be the first to notice and address problems. They should be a source of referral when the community is unsure what to do next.

CHECKLIST: placement

Family placements

Placements in families should be understood as re-creating a changed family and always needing safeguards.

- The placing event should a public occasion, taking time over it, talking through expectations on both sides.
- It should ask for confirmation in writing of the willingness to take the child.
- It should involve a community leader in a monitoring/advisory role.
- Inheritance issues may need to be addressed.
- It may also involve tracing staff follow-ups.

Kits

The role of kits should be considered with a decision on whether:

- to give a kit the community can benefit from;
- to give a kit the whole family can benefit from;
- to give a kit the child will benefit from;
- to give a small symbolic gift;
- not to give anything.

After-care

After-care decisions need to be made for every placement by asking what help a child needs to make a successful home in the particular situation. After-care help may involve counselling, help with accessing education or health, or more difficult questions of poverty.

Unable to place

Where families are unable or unwilling to have a child, the options that tracing staff should consider, should be spelt out in a policy document. Similarly, careful policy and practice guidance should be developed about responding to children who are unwilling to be reunified. Choice needs to be built into policy.

Substitute families

Placements with substitute families may be necessary as short-term placements during tracing or long-term placements where tracing has failed. Substitute family placements should consider:

- the motivation of the family;
- the standard of living of the family;
- the character of the family as seen by community members.

SUCCESS AND LEARNING

In this section we look at how we might measure success in a tracing pro-gramme and we conclude it is primarily a process of learning from the people involved. The first two sections look at ways of measuring success: follow-up visits to the children as a monitoring tool and evaluations as overall measures of the success of the project. The final part looks at the importance of working with and learning from communities to ensure success.

WHAT IS SUCCESS?

A key measure of success is the proper implementation of all stages of the tracing process. This includes:
- Proper planning and good management: resources, staff, training.
- Accurate assessment of the causes of the separation
  - through playing, talking, building a relationship with the child.
- Designing intelligent tracing plans and systems
  - developing excellent records of what the child wants, where the family might be and how best to find them.
- Assessing the family situation
  - assessing whether the family want to and can live with the child.
- Preparing the child
  - assessing whether the child wishes to live with the family and is well prepared and counselled.
- Reunifying, with active involvement from the community, or making alternative plans.
- Follow-up
  - including problem-solving and feedback to project.

Ways of increasing success:
- Forming a public education campaign around reunification.
- Promoting child/family contact before reunification.
- Involvement of community in planning, implementing, monitoring.
- Avoid top-down programmes.

- Staff to be carefully selected and committed. They must know the local culture and language.
- Clear guidelines.

FOLLOW-UP VISITS

Follow-up visits can be used to monitor the success of reunification. In emergency situations follow-up visits by people who are outside the receiving community are often not easily possible, especially if war conditions or population displacements continue. These external follow-up visits may also be expensive if children are very dispersed and not easily accessible. In practice follow-up visits are neither always accepted nor always implemented as an essential part of a family tracing programme.

Nevertheless follow-up visits remain part of good practice. Follow-up may be carried out by tracing workers who travel to the communities or by community leaders who live in the communities. The former may be more experienced at identifying problems, the latter are more experienced at using culturally appropriate ways of solving them. The disadvantage of the former is the cost, the disadvantage of the latter is the possible collusion of adults in a community against a child. But education is again the key – community leaders need to know how to follow up. For example the importance of speaking to children privately and the importance of listening and encouraging children to share their problems needs to be explicitly taught.

Children can also be asked to select someone to monitor the situation – a godparent, a chief, a teacher.

Examples of follow-up reports

Mary: Mary is 16 and fully resettled here. The parents are content, they say she is very useful and takes care of the younger ones. The programme is paying school fees. The family however looks very poor with poor shelter and clothing. I advised Mary to be serious in her studies and not to let her parents down. I cautioned her to be vigilant and avoid Aids.

Comment: Discussion with parents recorded. Observations and advice recorded. Child's own views not recorded.

Grace: Grace is 14 and lives with her maternal grandmother. She is well organised and works hard at school. The Resistance Committee Chairman says it is she who is the bread winner because she has her own gardens and her grandmother is too old to work them. She said she was happy to live at home.

Comment: Monitoring role of community leader noted, also child's own comments.

Rajeet: Rajeet is 13 and has run away from his grandfather three times. Each time he was brought back. He took time to resettle because he had been living in a town with excitements and the village way of life was hard for him. But now he says he is happy. He and his four brothers all sleep on one big mat.

Comment: Problem (running away) had been presented and interpreted (urban-rural change) and discussed. Appears to have got better with time.

Abdu: Abdu had been beating the younger children and refusing school. One of the fathers complained, the elders met and a spiritual healer was consulted. He said the spirit of the war was still in the child. A purification ceremony was arranged and the child is now calmer.

Comment: The community used its own cultural mechanism to interpret and respond to the problem.

How many visits?

How many follow-ups are necessary? Each situation is different. As a minimum we would suggest that each child should have one visit. This should not be a waste of resources, since the follow-up visit has the following functions:

- it enables the worker to assess the success of the reunification;
- it acts to prevent some problems, since both family and child are told and therefore expect that the situation will be followed up;
- it offers reassurance to the child, as all links to her past are not severed;
- it offers protection to the child, because when bad things do happen, there is someone who wants to know, who may be on her side;
- it offers problem-solving and negotiating skills, and an understanding of common problems that arise and solutions that can be tried;
- it offers feedback to the tracing programme on which aspects (i.e. preparation of child or family) need improving.

Families may be asked to bring a child weekly and then monthly to a clinic or social work office for a short visit. Or medical check-ups may be part of follow-ups, with health charts and weight charts filled in conscientiously. Other programmes may follow educational progress quite closely, offering financial help as long as the child continues to bring good reports from the school. Some programmes offer, and require, attendance at meetings. Others offer incentives for producing children for weighing and interviewing – such as bags of grain.

When to stop?

When to stop is a difficult question. Decisions need to relate to the aims of the programme, the degree of closeness of the family being reunified with and the conditions in the country. Where aims include continued educational help, for example, then it is the end of the education that marks the end of contact. Where aims are much more short term, then two to three months after a reunification may be an appropriate time to review it and conclude involvement.

- If the child is well settled, then one can expect future problems to be resolved in the same way that all community problems are.
- If the child is not well settled, then it is often a 'referral' to these problem-solving mechanisms that is needed. It is often a meeting of elders that is needed to put pressure on an uncle to stop beating a child or allowing her to go school.

It is often the involvement of traditional healers that is needed to help heal the nightmares and fears of children. But it is often political intervention that is needed when reunited children are then re-recruited into armies. Generally, however, children who are reunified with both their biological parents tend to need less follow-up than other children.

In one sense, follow-up is acting 'in loco parentis' – offering a small degree of protection and help particularly to children who do not live with the protection of their parents.

AN AUDIT OF PROBLEMS FOUND AT FOLLOW-UP STAGE

Some of the pressures and temptations for poorly paid tracing staff are:
- Some of the children's kits had been sold off by tracing staff instead of given to the children.
- Some of the tracing staff had beaten the children as punishment for running away.
- Police officers kept children they picked up for weeks, beat them and used them before they took them to court.
- Both reunification and follow-up forms had been completed for children who did not exist with false signatures.
- Children were not listened to and tracing staff and family adults made decisions without reference to the child.
- Reunification never took longer than 20 minutes, because tracing staff wanted to get home.
- Social workers were paid by parents to send children to orphanages, or to approved schools to enable relatives to access the land children had inherited.
- Tracing staff accepted financial gifts to arrange reunifications which were happening anyway.

EVALUATION

Evaluations focus on the success of the whole tracing programme. Evaluations have to address two issues. On the one hand there is the efficiency of the programme – the practices and procedures followed, whether those were adequate, whether they were cost-effective, whether they can be improved, speeded up, done differently. On the other hand there is the effectiveness of the programme – what impact has it had on the children and families and communities? Have families welcomed the children, nurtured them, helped them to adapt to the new separation and the reunification? Have children been well prepared? Or, alternatively, have families felt the programme dumped children on them against their will; have children felt they have been treated as objects delivered to unwilling adults?

Indicators of success or failure can be developed. For example:
- what proportion of children have run away, have suffered from malnutrition, have stopped attending school although they had attended prior to reunification?;

- what proportion of children say they feel sad, unloved and wish they were somewhere else?;
- what proportion of children have not had family traced and not had any long-term planning done for their future?

It is the combination of good practice in procedures and good practice outcomes which must demonstrate the success or failure of the programme. And it must be the children and the communities judging it.

COMMON IMPEDIMENTS TO A SUCCESSFUL PROGRAMME

Bad planning

- insufficient budgeting to do it well;
- aims not clear;
- badly managed;
- methods not clear: process vs event, talking at vs listening to child;
- relationship between programme and government not well defined: either too separate or too close and politicised;
- staff not trained, not paid, not motivated;
- trying to do it too fast and not taking time to prepare children, involve communities or educate families;
- emphasising numbers reunified at the expense of the quality of the process and the impact on the communities and the child.

Badly carried out assessment

- children quizzed without fully understanding what is happening to them;
- children's fears not discussed;
- children not asked whom they would like to live with.

Bad tracing system

- inadequate forms which do not ask the right questions;
- staff who do not use or understand the forms;
- carelessness in completing them, keeping & analysing them;
- expensive trips carried out without local knowledge or community involvement;
- children involved in tracing trips without preparation, without regard to how they feel, without counselling;
- choosing who gets reunified first by preferential treatment to children from a particular ethnic group or region. Deliberately leaving some last or some untraced.

Dumping children

- leaving children even when families do not want them;
- leaving children even when they clearly do not wish to stay and no one has established why;
- leaving children without any safeguards built into the plan;
- not handing over an agreed kit;
- asking for payment from the family.

Inadequate follow-up

- no follow-up;
- follow-up which only listens to adults;
- follow-up which does not address post-placement needs;
- follow-up which does not recognise mistakes made and does not feed back information on them.

No review/evaluation

- no learning or improvement possible.

COMMUNITY LEADERS – AN ESSENTIAL INGREDIENT OF SUCCESS

"In the past we tended to think we could move mountains and have solutions to everything. We imposed solutions on individuals and communities. We have now learned. Our role as professionals is not to make the decisions, but to help communities make the decisions and care for their children."

A tracing worker looking back

Community leaders are increasingly seen as key people in tracing programmes. Early programmes sometimes worked without them: specialist tracers/local social workers returned children to individually named family members. Then gradually the importance of community leaders began to emerge.

They are key informants in tracing, some holding entire histories of community members in their memories. They open doors for tracing staff to travel, to visit, to ask questions. They facilitate meetings, their support reassures people and increases their participation. Their presence at reunification makes obligations clear and promises serious. Their monitoring role creates an accountability for parenting which is local, immediate and culturally appropriate.

It does not of course always work. Communities may be dispersed, dislocated, battered and desperate. Community leaders may be too busy, too far, too weak, insensitive to children or just corrupt. Training is one of the important ways of addressing these problems, helping people in the local community to understand the children, even when they appear quiet and withdrawn or angry and defiant, to identify the causes of the problem, and to react constructively. Professionals learning from, working with, and building partnerships with community leaders is a key component of the success of a tracing programme.

Indeed there is overwhelming evidence that families search for children through their own networks whether or not there is a tracing programme, and that informal systems of message sending, information gathering and family searching co-exist with every formal system. The challenge here is to identify these systems, strengthen them and build on them. Having two tracing systems, which never learn from each other, which are never accessed by the same people, operating in one country at the same time, does not add to overall effectiveness. But having two tracing methods: the files in the capital or the computer print out which is updated monthly *and* the message to the chief of the village 500 kms away relayed on market days by people of the same clan, may double the chances of a child finding their family or a parent finding their child. Communities are resources to use, they have skills which need to be developed, they are essential partners in tracing activities.

COMMUNITY LEADERS IN UGANDA

The Resistance Committee (RC) is the elected local government structure. It is elected at village level and plays a very important role: executive, legislative and judicial. It deals with children's matters (child protection, abuse, neglect) although it has no special powers to do so.

Anyone returning a child should inform an RC member and ask him to keep an eye on the child. "This is your child now. He is a member of your village. Look after him." He is left a stamped and addressed envelope to report problems that cannot be solved at RC level.

STAFF AND TRAINING

RECRUITMENT

One of the themes that comes up with every review or evaluation of a tracing programme is the crucial importance of effective staff: staff who work with children and communities and staff who work on planning and management. Tracing is an extraordinarily difficult task to carry out, because it involves a combination of such different skills. It involves being child-centred and child-sensitive yet also bureaucratic with attention to detail; it requires lateral thinking in piecing together bits of information as well as routine perseverance in cross-checking information.

Some programme planners argue that these tasks can only be carried out by trained social workers. Others argue that many countries have few or no trained social workers and reliance on those would prevent the development of any tracing programme. There seems sense in both arguments: recruiting social workers means that there should be a head start on some of the training issues like listening to children; but selection on motivation and skills remains necessary. Recruiting people who have other experience and are motivated and capable may mean a longer learning period but possibly an equally successful programme. Some of the essential staff ingredients are discussed below.

Child sensitivity

What does this mean in practice?

- Tracing staff need to be able to play with a doll with three- or four-year-olds, asking the child what happened to the doll's mummy and where did the doll live before she came here.
- Tracing staff need to be able to play football with nine-year-olds, organise them into teams and explore regional identification issues through the competitive spirit generated.
- Tracing staff need the skills to develop trusting relationships with children who are blind or deaf or dumb; children who have lost limbs and hope and trust.

Administrative skills

The same staff, or at least some staff in the tracing programme, need to be able to spend hours copying out information on to forms. This may need to be done in the midst of fighting or in the centre of camps surrounded with dying children or in orphanages where care staff define tracing staff as thieves taking their livelihood away from them. They need nevertheless to continue copying from forms on to different forms, possibly then on to computers, when these stop functioning then looking up details on lists and cross-referring manually adults with children and children with possible siblings and children with dates of birth and dates of separation with community leaders and so on.

The value of proven experience

Is this really feasible? Yes, in many places it is. Some of the places where it has worked best is where people are chosen from camps where they are already working with children and have demonstrated the motivation and capacity to engage and debate and play and listen and guide and reassure and encourage. In other places some relevant experience needs to be there.

Temporary recruitment

Recruitment should always be temporary at first, to make sure that the programme has the best kind of staff and does not have to compromise its objectives because the staff were badly chosen. A month or three months probationary period allows tracing staff to demonstrate their skills and either stay, as committed and effective tracers, or leave as not-quite-up-to the high standards required. Needless to say, where the only qualification people have is being related to someone important, this is insufficient reason to think they can do the job.

Willingness to persevere and to travel

Having grappled with children and administration, the next step is to set out for long and uncertain trips, up the mountains or into the deserts or into areas where the enemy still rule or the battle still continues. These trips are by definition dangerous, uncertain and difficult, and no matter how many four-wheel drive vehicles the NGOs make available, they do not protect against road mines or snipers or the distrust of the distant communities. When tracing staff arrive, they need the confidence to search market places and town halls and district administrators and village headmen; to work with interpreters and often with the hostility and fear and anger of a population that wants food rather than questions.

TRAINING AND MANAGING

Much of this ability, this confidence mixed with sensitivity, must be present from the start, as must the motivation to keep going when the chances of finding anyone are slim. And then, on top of this, training is required.

Ideally training will follow a training needs analysis, which will identify the main features of a particular tracing programme, package these into 'training modules' and present them in a mixture of open learning and taught day courses on 'effective tracing'. A manual, adapted to the particular political situation, culture and disaster needs also to be prepared. Having standard letters, forms and systems in place also facilitates the learning task of tracers.

And strong management, which reviews progress, identifies weaknesses and provides guidance may be the key to it all.

Accountability with money

What is it spent on, who decides, who oversees it? In desperately poor countries it is possible that money becomes diverted from tracing to raising the living standards of tracers or influential people in the community. But it is also possible that inflexible budgets prevent initiative and innovation, hinder progress, and dependency on technology such as films prevents any progress being made.

Ethical accountability with the programme

Wars and even natural disasters often become politicised in many ways. Where different tribal groups or religious groups are involved, it is sometimes difficult for professionals among them to stay 'professionally' neutral. The professionals' own children may have been killed by people from the 'other side'. How does one respond to 'their' children?

While there needs to be sympathy for all individuals who have been hurt by wars and by the divisions which follow, it is vitally important that tracing programmes do not get caught up in this. Children from all groups need to be treated the same way; children from 'enemy' territory need the same services; children who have fought still need protection; children with different religions or language or features need families as much as others. This should be part of the professional ethics of a programme. It is a management responsibility that this message is clearly understood and implemented.

Staff management

Staff are the most important resource in this programme, and they need to be well managed and supported. This means setting very high standards and rewarding them. If it is normal practice for professionals in other jobs to come to work late, not do very much and leave early in order to see to some private business, then alternative high standards have to be forged, fostered, insisted on and expected. When met, they need to be rewarded; and this means developing some incentive system which gets staff on the road as much as possible. It is still, unfortunately, money which rewards people's effort and tracing staff who are good at a difficult job need to be paid in a way that acknowledges this and that prevents them needing to have other jobs concurrently. If this creates an anomaly or a precedent, this may well be necessary. The short-term nature of the work, the dangers inherent it, the productivity expected can all be used as justifications. But the system can only work if staff can be removed from the tracing programme if underperforming.

EIGHTEEN EXAMPLES OF POSSIBLE STAFFING ISSUES

- People don't turn up for work.
- People are only willing to work with people of their own tribe/religion.
- Cars are stolen and mobility constrained.
- A social worker is anyone who happens to be employed in that ministry or orphanage.
- Staff in orphanages and tracing teams refuse to cooperate.
- Staff in orphanages instruct children not to tell the truth.
- Kits are sold off by tracing workers because their wages are so low.
- Tracing staff make it known to families that they expect personal gifts for the return of their children; and only those who are able and willing will see their children.
- Staff have not been paid for months – because no government employees have.
- National staff do not like travelling to provinces.
- Even in provinces tracing is not done because sitting in an office is easier than travelling.
- Follow-up is not done because staff do not believe in it.
- Practically no training takes place at district level.
- Files sit on desks for months and no one opens them.
- No management is expected or found.
- Documentation is not done because there are no forms or films; no one has ordered them and no one thinks to work without them.
- Tracing is not done because there is no petrol and no one wants to travel by bus or truck.

POLITICS AND PARTNERSHIPS

This section discusses ways that national governments and non-governmental organisations (NGOs) can work together on developing a tracing programme. This is a partnership which may take various forms and which grows out of wider political and developmental considerations. Some of these questions have been raised as part of the who-should-do-the-tracing question. But here the wider implications are drawn out.

THE POLITICS OF EFFICIENCY

On the one hand, there is a partnership model which emphasises internal efficiency: NGOs will tend to initiate such a programme and allocate a budget and staff. Partnership with government may be little more than keeping them informed of the overall aims. Consultation on whether such a programme is a priority one or whether the methods proposed are effective, is not likely to take place. Ownership of the programme will be clearly in the hands of the NGO, as will the material collected and research undertaken.

This kind of project is likely to:

- appoint its own field level staff;
- make them accountable to the project staff, possibly to expatriate staff;
- have employment conditions and pay better than those of locally employed staff;
- liaise badly with government departments;
- use 'outside' concepts such as western ideas of professionalism, of accountability, of value for money;
- apply western concepts of choice and individualism.

This model is likely to create a knowledgeable specialist core team of workers and lead to high numbers of children being traced and reunified in relatively short periods of time. Thus the internal efficiency of the project will be high. On the other hand, the project will fit uneasily with other kinds of development which is carried out with or closer to government departments. The project may elicit considerable resentment from colleagues and disapproval from government. Various attempts to obstruct it may follow. It may run parallel to, and seemingly in competition with, ministries of social welfare or departments of social work. It may have four-wheel drive cars, petrol and inflated salaries, while public sector social workers may have none of these. And perhaps most importantly, in the long run it will contribute nothing to the public sector service which will continue, badly resourced, under-motivated and inefficient, untouched by the fast stream service invested in parallel.

THE POLITICS OF LONG-TERM EFFECTIVENESS

On the other hand, the partnership model being developed may be at the other end of the partnership continuum. The NGO may decide:
- to work very closely with government;
- to invest the money directly into a government department;
- to use existing staff and lines of management to carry out the work.

In such a project, for example, existing government staff may be expected to carry out tracing activities, having been trained by NGO staff, carrying the work out to standards developed by the NGO and with dual or unclear accountability.

In the short term, this is likely to mean tracing activity competes with other responsibilities and less tracing is done than if the staff were specialist ones. Numbers will be low, demand will remain high. At the same time, the competition for priority may be felt by both staff and management who may resent changing their work, their priorities, their methods, for an external organisation. From their point of view, they are not being paid more than they were. It may also seem like the Ministry has been 'bought' and its priorities hijacked and diverted by foreign currency and foreign nationals. And many social workers may well feel that the bulk of their work as provincial or district staff becomes neglected. In the short term all these issues have to be recognised and worked through.

In the long term, however, there are likely to be benefits. The training and the general review of work practices and methods is relatively transferable. Thus what is learnt and how it is learnt should be useful for much of social work or community work and for much general administration and development work. In this sense, what in the short term is continued competition and negotiation is, in the long run, an investment in the skills and the capabilities of government departments. If and when an NGO pulls out and withdraws money, tracing is likely to continue, the experienced staff are still there and the forms and the system might survive.

THE MIXED ECONOMY OF WELFARE

Is there a way of developing a partnership which builds on the advantages of both models? One option has been to start with the former model and then move, after the staff intensive development stage, to the latter. This is the reverse move of those advocating privatisation of many government services and this may require some explanation. While there is an emergency, government departments are very stretched, often concerned with bare survival of the population, and tracing is an irrelevant luxury. At that stage tracing needs to be 'privatised' – privately funded, designed, provided. NGOs are in one sense private organisations, substituting their values and ideologies for the profit motive. And, as most private companies, NGOs too reach the stage where the project is no longer viable – not with profit but with their definition of needs and priorities and they move on to other projects or other countries. At that stage, government is left with the work that still needs to be done. The reverse of privatisation seems an inevitable development in tracing work growing out of emergencies. Perhaps, in the long run, it can combine the initial high quality, high quantity service for children with longer-term investment in governmental responsibilities and governmental skills in meeting them.

AN EXAMPLE WHERE TRACING WAS PRIVATISED

"We had been doing it for nine months, working in the midst of the war, designing our own methodology and learning every day. We had a lot of meetings, so that all the staff could feed back what was happening, and we could learn from each other. And then 'they' came in and took it over from us. They said we were a bunch of illiterates and we could not possibly run such a programme. We were 'local staff' and not professionals. It was an interesting dichotomy – we couldn't be both local and professionals. That was a contradiction in terms. And do you know what the professional's profession was? One was a geography graduate and the other had a degree in animal husbandry. Both were new to the country. Why are these considered professionals? We had been doing tracing for nine months; had reunified nearly a thousand children; we knew the languages, the customs, the area. But they were the professionals."

A local tracing manager reminiscing

THE POLITICS OF GOVERNMENT SOCIAL WORK

"We mostly work with NGOs now. Five or six years ago the government stopped allocating resources to us. The government stills employs us, but we do what the NGOs offer us. Because we have no budget from government we cannot initiate anything. Before, we used to have our own priorities, our own methods, our own plans. But all that's gone. We have learnt how to change from being active to being passive; from initiating projects to responding to them. Now we wait for NGOs to suggest projects, to contact the Minister. Then we both get a letter of agreement and understanding. We now only work on implementation."

Government social worker

DEVELOPMENT

Much of this guide has been concerned with tracing as an emergency programme in wars and disasters. Family tracing however remains relevant in times of peace and planned social and economic development. In this section we give some brief examples of how family tracing may remain a cornerstone of social policy with regard to children.

STREET CHILDREN

Street children are some of the most vulnerable urban children in many developing countries. They are highly visible – living or working on the streets from an early age. They are highly vulnerable – in many countries open to abuse by adults and in some countries facing violent deaths. They are often labelled as 'undesirable' having been drawn into crime or prostitution.

For many of the younger children, family tracing offers a way off the streets and back to the rural areas the families or children came from. For many of the older children, reunification is not enough. These children are now earners and the question is how to support this role with less dangerous activities, not how to reverse it. This applies as much to boys in Brazil as girls in Thailand. The after-care issues and follow-up remain important.

However, for all children the principles and values of tracing remain important:

- Children should have a right to have a family, whether or not they live with them.
- If children cannot live with them, they should have a right to an 'interview' to discuss where they could live and where they would like to live and what could be done to facilitate this.
- Children should have choices about where they will live, and not just be rounded up by police or government in various 'clean city' operations.

These principles can be the cornerstone for working with street children. It is clear from research that many forcibly returned separated children, end up as street children. And many street children are separated children, from family displacements and acute poverty. The two are closely linked.

ORPHANAGES

Countries vary in the degree to which they actively support institutional care for children. However, most do still have historically inherited children's homes set up by missionaries or colonial governments, by aid agencies such as SOS Villages or by Presidents' wives.

What should they do with them? These institutions attract money, and are often able to provide relatively high material standards – at least in the urban areas. Some give the children milk when no one else has access to milk; the EC milk surplus gets diverted to the orphanage. Diplomats' wives, unable to get work permits, may set themselves the unpaid task of reorganising orphanages to provide more western type of care with toys, playground equipment, children's furnishings. Some institutions may set extremely high western standards of environment and housing, which ministers' children rather than orphans may wish to access.

But the evidence of the damaging effects of these institutions continues to grow. They cannot substitute for families; they cannot socialise children with the appropriate cultural role models; they cannot create secure identities from within institutional boundaries. They may not teach children to cook or sew or their age-appropriate cultural behaviour. Institutional children are often considered rude or ignorant; unable to share and take on responsibilities; excessively self-centred with assumptions of rights to beds or privacy or time of their own which no other child of the same age would have. Many have major problems surviving outside their institutions, after having left.

One of the greatest long-term benefits most of these institutionalised children need, is family tracing. Even if they are not removed from the home, but merely enabled to visit extended family during holidays, this is nevertheless usually enough to create a whole new dimension to their identity: it provides roots. It anchors them in a way that no amount of money can. It gives them a security to fall back on to if the promises of institutional life do not materialise when they leave. Family tracing opens doors.

CHILD PROSTITUTION

In some parts of the world, child prostitution is much more common than it is in the five countries that have been studied for this guide. The wider evidence suggests that many of the issues about separation – the trauma, the loss, the mourning of the family, the wishing but fearing to go home, are all common features of situations where children may have been sold into prostitution as an anti-poverty strategy of the family.

Programmes trying to respond to the 'best interests' of those children face similar problems of trying to trace families and negotiating with families who have been traced. What choices do those children have and how can social interventions help? There are also increasing problems with HIV/Aids, where some countries will not accept the return of HIV/Aids children, while in others there is a lot of stigma and very little help for the dying children. Tracing, assessment and substitute placements remain important features of a child protection programme for child prostitutes, whether the children are in South America or South Asia.

POLICY AND LAW

Family tracing work needs to be underpinned by a clearly articulated social policy based on an updated legal framework. Too often countries have inherited a colonial legal framework which is completed outdated; its values are not current ones; its emphasis on penal responses to problems may be the reverse of what is needed; its range of policy instruments is restricted and inadequate. Law reform offers new directions, new standards, new debate about children's needs and rights. This is not the place to discuss what it can and can't achieve – suffice it to say that family tracing is both reaching back to traditional values of the importance of families and communities reclaiming their children, but also reaching forward to the debate on children's rights and indicators which will identify progress on these rights. The right to a family is more fundamental than many other rights, and also, much more easily measurable. We are back to seeing family tracing as a bridge between relief and development, and successful family living as an indicator of progress for children and as an achievable aim of development.

APPENDIX 1: Examples of forms

This appendix lays out *examples* of family tracing forms used in different countries. They would need to be adapted to be used by others.

Child case record: Uganda

UGANDA

The Approved Schools (Children's Homes) Rules, 1991

FORM 3: CHILD CASE RECORD

Part I – Initial record

Name of children's home _____

Name of child _____ Age _____

Date of birth _____ Religion _____

Date of admission _____ Sex _____

Type of order _____

Father's name _____ Alive/Dead _____

Occupation _____

Address _____

Mother's name _____ Alive/Dead _____

Occupation _____

Address _____

Name of brothers and sisters and where they are living:

Name _____ Address _____

Name _____ Address _____

Name _____ Address _____

Name _____ Address _____

Other important relatives, foster parents, guardians:

Name   Relationship   Address

_____

_____

_____

_____

Child's school _____ Class _____

Child case record: Uganda *(continued)*

Are holidays spent with parents or relations? _____

Is there contact with parents, relations or others in home community? _____

Details of disability or handicap: _____

Circumstances leading to admission to the home: _____

Future plans: _____

Other relevant information eg property owned by child: _____

Name and status of person completing the record: _____

Signature _____ Date _____

Reunification form: Uganda

DETAILS OF CHILD RESETTLED WITH PARENTS OR RELATIVES
BY DISTRICT PROBATION AND WELFARE OFFICERS

Station _____

Name of child _____ Age _____ Sex _____

Institution if in one before resettled _____

_____ Date resettled _____

Type of case – beyond control, care and protection, criminal (detail offence), no order

_____

Name of person with whom child resettled _____

Address _____

_____

Relationship to child _____

Signature of recipient _____

Name and village of RC chairman _____

Signature of RC representative _____

Tracing officer's name _____

Items of self sufficiency kit given _____

_____

_____

_____

Comments _____

_____

_____

_____ Date of next visit _____

Comments on second visit _____

_____

NB: If there is need for further visits put overleaf

Reminder: 1) A copy of this form is to be sent to the Inspection and Statistics Unit.
           2) A stamped self–addressed envelope should be left with the RC representative contacted.

Follow-up report form: Uganda

RESETTLEMENT FOLLOW-UP REPORT

Name of child _____ Age _____ Sex _____

Institution child resettled from _____

Address of resettled child: (ie RC 1 village, sub–county, county, district) _____

_____

_____

Please answer the following questions:

1. How does the child say he/she feels about being back with their relatives? _____

_____

_____

_____

2. Does the child appear to be healthy? If not, state the problem. _____

_____

_____

_____

3. What is the reaction of the parents/guardians to having the child with them? _____

_____

_____

_____

4. Is the child in school? If so, give the name of the school and the class. _____

_____

_____

_____

5. If the child is not in school does the child feel he/she is usefully occupied? State
what the child is doing. _____

_____

_____

_____

Follow-up report form: Uganda *(continued)*

6. How does the RC member who knows the child think the child is settling down in the family and community? _____ _____

_____

7. Are the home conditions of the child satisfactory ie adequate shelter, clothes, a mat and bedding? _____

_____

8. Write down whatever advice, guidance and support you have given to the family and child during your follow–up visit. _____

_____

_____

_____

_____

9. Any other matter that is significant and relevant. _____

_____

_____

_____

Print your name _____ Print your district _____

Your signature _____ Date of report _____

NB: Please obtain a signature from an RC I member who you have spoken to concerning the child.

Signature and stamp of RC I member _____

Date signed _____

Life history form: Liberia

LIBERIA

LIFE HISTORY FORM

Name _____ Also known as _____

Date of birth _____ Age _____

Sex _____ Place of birth _____

Nationality _____ Tribe _____

Religious affiliation _____

Languages spoken _____

Last permanent address _____

Last school attended _____

Grade completed _____

Colour of skin _____ Colour of hair _____

Colour of eyes _____ Marks of identification _____

_____

Height _____ Weight _____

Place where child was found _____

Date _____ Time (be exact) _____

Names of people that accompanied child   Relationship

_____

_____

_____

What does the child think happened to them _____

_____

Circumstances of their separation? _____

_____

Reasons for separation _____

_____

Under what conditions did the child last see his/her parents/guardian or other family member: _____

Life history form: Liberia (continued)

Does the child think they are alive/dead? _____ _____

Recall date and time of separation: Date ___ _____ Time _____

Did the parents/guardian depart from child, or did the child depart from parents? ___

Was this separation forced or voluntary? _____

If family was travelling, where were they going? _____

Give direction _____

Was the child with any other person/group who might offer some information about him/her? _____

Where can this person be found? _____

What was their relationship to the child? _____

How did they get together? _____

How long did they stay together? _____

Family chart

Name	Age	Sex	Last known address	Place of work	Com.

Life history form: Liberia *(continued)*

History of child before and after separation

After separation from parents, where did you go? _____

_____

How long did you stay there? _____

Where were you after separation? _____

Medical and health record

Have you had any health problems? _____

_____

Which one? _____

Record information about immunisation that the child has had before _____

_____

Describe child's physical/emotional state _____

_____

To what extent are the child's needs being met and how? _____

_____

How has the child adjusted to his/her present situation and how has he/she integrated

into it? _____

_____

Other relevant information

Do you have any special problems/needs? _____

_____

With whom does the child wish to be reunified? _____

_____

Relationship _____

Last permanent address _____

Name of social worker _____

Date of interview _____ Place of interview _____

International Committee of the Red Cross: form used in Liberia

International Committee of the Red Cross

NON ACCOMPANIED CHILDREN

Date _____ Place _____

1. Registered child

Full name _____ M / F

Age _____ _____ Tribe _____ Nationality _____

Last address _____

2. Names of eventual accompanying persons

Names of eventual accompanying persons	Age	Family relation	M / F

3. Parents

Father's name _____ Deceased / Missing

Mother's name _____ Deceased / Missing

Last known address _____

4. Other relatives

Names and address of other relatives able to provide some information — Might take care of the child

	Might take care of the child
_____	Yes / No
_____	Yes / No
_____	Yes / No
_____	Yes / No
_____	Yes / No

International Committee of the Red Cross: Liberia form (continued)

---

5. Person who found the child

Full name _____

Address _____

Information about the place where the child was found:

(where? in which circumstances? when? with whom?)

_____

_____

_____

_____

_____

6. Address of the orphanage/or other place of residence

Person in charge _____

Address _____

7. Transfer

Family in charge_____

Contact address _____

8. Remarks

_____

_____

_____

_____

_____

9. DEQ for: Name _____

Relative link _____

Cote _____

Resettlement form: Liberia

LIBERIA
RESETTLEMENT FORM

Name of child _____ Age _____ Sex _____

Name of institution where child has been living _____

Name of person with whom child resettled _____

Relationship of person to child _____

Physical address _____

Items given to child: _____

_____

_____

_____

_____

_____

_____

Signature/Thumb print of child _____

Signature/Thumb print of parent/relative/guardian _____

Signature/Thumb print of witness from the community _____

Comments on resettlement: _____

_____

_____

_____

_____

Date of follow–up visit agreed with child _____

Name of person who carried out the resettlement _____

Signature _____ Date _____

APPENDIX 2: Further reading

Guides

H Tefferi: *Family Reunification in Drought Affected Areas,* Radda Barnen, Ethiopia 1990.

J Williamson & A Moser: *Unaccompanied Children in Emergencies,* International Social Services, 1987.

N Richman & D Pereira: *Helping Children in Difficult Circumstances, A Teacher's Manual,* SCF 1991.

N **Richman:** *Communicating with Children: Helping Children in Distress,* SCF 1993.

Evaluations

E Green, J Williamson, P Nimpuno-Parente: *Evaluation of the Children and War Program,* SCF-US, 1992.